# FALKLANDS:
## TASK FORCE
## PORTFOLIO
### PART 2

**Edited by Mike Critchley**

**Introduced by Admiral of the Fleet
Sir Terence Lewin G.C.B., M.V.O., D.S.C.**

£4.50

# EDITORS NOTE

When the security screen was lifted from the South Atlantic operations information and photographs "flooded in" for this second part of our Task Force Portfolio. It came from South Thule to Scotland.

It has been an enormous task to try to tell the story of the Task Force "in action" in any form of chronological order—so many events were going on at the same time—involving all arms of the services. I have thus completed this edition in basically three sections to cover action on—land, at sea—and in the air—before the final victory. The book ends with with a look at the Falklands in the days after the Argentine surrender and the forces return home.

Most of the words and photographs are from men of the Task Force and our thanks must go to them all—too numerous to name—for their two fingered efforts on a typewriter on their journey home.

I have attempted to give a fair spread to all the units involved in the South Atlantic operations from the material submitted. Regretfully I have had to discard material that could fill another 3 books!

An enormous amount of 'midnight oil' has been burnt assembling this book but I have felt compelled to record these fantastic events—as seen by the men themselves—before the whole operation fades from the nation's memory. No attempt has been made to criticise men or equipment—despite the opportunity to do so. Hindsight can be a wonderful thing . . .

It has been a remarkable experience talking to many of the people involved in the operation whilst compiling this book (from Senior Officers to Falkland shopkeepers). I only hope this end result will help to remind us all in coming years of these memorable events in the South Atlantic.

For many who lost loved ones—the action can never be forgotten. Many of the hundreds of men wounded will have to bear the scars of war forever—and will, regretfully, soon be forgotten as "yesterday's heroes".

I only hope this book, in some small way, will be a fitting tribute to them all . . .

*Mike Critchley*

**Mike Critchley**
**Looe**
**Cornwall**

We have decided to donate a considerable proportion of any profit from the sale of this book, to the King Georges Fund for Sailors which has a magnificent record of caring for seafarers and their families over the last century—and will play a major role in caring for those on whom this operation will leave a permanent scar.

**By**
**Admiral of the Fleet Lord Lewin**
**G.C.B., M.V.O., D.S.C.**
**Chief of the Defence Staff 1979-1982**

I admired Part One of the Falklands Task Force Portfolio and am particularly pleased to have been asked to write the foreword to Part Two. As the campaign in the South Atlantic begins to fade into history, the books that porport to give an especially knowledgeable account are appearing in numbers. Inevitably, because the authors could not have full access to the whole range of intelligence and information, they have put their own interpretation on events as they saw them. Many of them are, in places, inaccurate and misleading. Task Force Portfolio is different. It tells the story graphically, accurately and without opinionative embroidery. It is brilliantly illustrated, as was Part One, with photographs from a wide range of professional and amateur service photographers.

As the account unfolds, you will see clearly that this was a campaign in which each of our three Services and the Merchant Service played its vital part, and its success was an object lesson in joint planning and co-operation. But even more clearly will you see that the final victory was won by the quality and dedication of our people, from those at home who gave so much support to those in the fighting line. The whole country can take pride in the achievement of the Task Force. We have demonstrated that agression cannot be allowed to succeed, and that we have the courage to fight for freedom.

*Terence Lewin*

**Admiral of the Fleet**

# THE STORY SO FAR—A SOUTH ATLANTIC DIARY

PART 1 of this book covered the first part of the Falklands crisis. A brief history is given below.

**March 19**—Scrap-metal workers, hired to dismantle a disused whaling station, land without British consent at Leith, South Georgia and hoist the Argentine flag.

**April 2**—Argentine troops invade the Falkland Islands from the sea.
   Massive operations start to prepare the Task Force.

**April 4**—United Nations condemns Argentine aggression and calls for withdrawal of troops. South Georgia falls after fierce battle with the small Royal Marines contingent.

**April 5**—Lord Carrington resigns as Foreign Secretary. First ships in Britain's task force sail.

**April 6**—U.S. Secretary of State, Alexander Haig, starts peace-seeking mission. Mr. Francis Pym appointed Foreign Secretary.

**April 8**—Britain declares a 200 mile exclusion zone around Falklands with effect from April 12. Argentine Junta responds with its own South Atlantic operations zone.

**April 9**—P & O liner Canberra sails from Southampton for the war zone.

**April 16**—Task force sails from Ascension Island after brief stop-over, for the South Atlantic.

**April 21**—First contact between Task Force and Argentinians—Royal Navy Sea Harrier intercepts and warns off Boeing 707 "Snooping" over the Force.

**April 22**—Two helicopters crash on South Georgia as SBS unit is put ashore. No casualties.

**April 25**—South Georgia recaptured with no British casualties. M. Company 42 Commando RM first ashore as Major Guy Sheridan leads two hour operation. Argentine submarine Santa Fe crippled. About 190 prisoners are taken.

**April 26**—Lt Cdr Alfredo Astiz signs document of surrender of South Georgia.

**April 28**—Blockade around Falklands extended by Britain to exclude aircraft of all nations as well as ships.

**April 30**—Argentina declares 200-mile "no-go" zone covering same area as Britain's total exclusion zone.

**May 1**—Haig peace mission ends in failure. United States at last decides to join EEC countries to back Britain with economic sanctions—and offers military supplies.
   Sea Harriers shoot down one Mirage fighter and one Canberra bomber. Second Mirage accidentally shot down by Argentine aircraft. HMS Arrow slightly damaged. RAF Vulcan bomber craters Port Stanley airfield, Sea Harriers follow up with bomb and rocket attacks around Port Stanley and Goose Green air-strips.
   Cunards flagship, Queen Elizabeth 2 is requisitioned as a troop carrier.

**May 2**—Argentine cruiser, the General Belgrano, sunk by torpedoes fired by HMS Conqueror 36 miles outside the "total exclusion" zone.

**May 3**—Lynx helicopters attack two Somoto-class tug gun boats with Sea Skua missiles after the vessels had fired on Sea Kings from HMS Hermes. Comodoro Somellera is sunk and Alferez badly damaged.

**May 4**—Lt Nicholas Taylor RN is killed when his Sea Harrier is shot down during attack on Goose Green airfield. RAF Vulcan again bombs Port Stanley runway.
   HMS Sheffield, is hit by an Exocet missile fired by an Argentine aircraft. 20 men died, 24 injured.

**May 6**—Contact lost with two Sea Harriers. Pilots Lt Cdr John Eyton-Jones and Lt William Curtis missing presumed dead. Peace efforts led by Peru end in failure.

**May 7**—Britain widens war zone to within 12 nautical miles of Argentina's coast. New peace initiative is launched by United Nations Secretary-General, Javier Perez de Cuellar.

**May 9**—Narwal, an Argentine fishing vessel said to have been used as spy ship, is strafed by two Royal Navy Sea Harriers. One member of the crew is killed and 13 injured. Narwal boarded but later sinks. An Argentine helicopter is shot down by a missile from a British warship. Army Garrison around Port Stanley bombarded by British warships.

**May 10**—Argentine supply ship shelled and blown up by HMS Alactrity operating for first time inside the Falkland Sound between the two main islands. HMS Sheffield sinks while under tow to safe anchorage in South Georgia.

**May 11**—Argentinian Puma helicopter shot down. Warships bombard Port Stanley troop installations again.

**May 12**—Queen Elizabeth 2 sails from Southampton for the war zone. Four Argentine Sky Hawk fighter bombers escorting flights into the Falklands are shot down. Argentine aircraft holes a British destroyer with a bomb which does not explode.

As events deteriorate in the South Atlantic the first British casualty of the war—HMS Sheffield—is towed towards a safe anchorage by HMS YARMOUTH. It was to be a short tow—she soon sank—and remains a war grave in the vast expanses of the South Atlantic.

# NO TURNING BACK . . . !

With South Georgia back in British hands morale couldn't have been higher throughout the Task Force. Last minute planning details were finalised as the ships drew close to the Falklands. The diplomats failed to reach an acceptable compromise, only one option remained—invasion.

Young men of 40 Commando, some fresh out of training, prepare for the dawn assult in one of the many ships moving towards the coast.

Deep in the Magazine of HMS Plymouth—as she approached San Carlos water—men, unaware of what future hours would bring, reduce the tension by playing the age old messdeck game of "Uckers" (Ludo) surrounded by live ammunition.

# THE LAND WAR . . .

As the amphibious force approached San Carlos Water the special forces (who had been ashore since the beginning of May) marked the beaches for the first landing craft. Their reconnaissance had checked for mines and enemy troops.

The landing craft moved through the darkness as destroyers and frigates saturated targets with gunfire to provide diversions. On Fanning Head a group of Argentine troops were attacked by the SBS. At dawn the enemy withdrew but whilst doing so shot down two Gazelle helicopters (possibly using British built Blowpipe missiles), killing some of the crews. Nine prisoners, who were described as 'cold, wet and miserable', were taken.

The SAS downed the first Argentine aircraft to attack—a Pucara. By midday the air attacks began in earnest. They were to continue for several days. Slowly the air defences around San Carlos were improved, the Blowpipes were supplemented by Rapier, and a Combat Air Patrol provided from ships further out to the East. The area was soon christened as "Bomb Alley" by the ships as daily bombings from the Argentines became "routine". All the ships in the loch bristled with machine guns on ad hoc mounts so that any pilot arriving in the area was guaranteed the widest range of armament to be awaiting him. First kills to the Rapier System were when 33 Charlie of T. Battery (Shah Sujah's Troop) took two Skyhawks from the sky.

LCUs from HMS Fearless ferry Commandos to the San Carlos beaches.

Amongst the first ashore were men of 3 Para. They are pictured here leaving their LCVPs and fanning out in a tactical formation soon after dawn.

Royal Marines of 45 Cdo dig in and prepare defensive positions at Ajax Bay.

The problems that confronted the Surface to Air missile crews were similar to those facing the Argentine pilots. The shape of San Carlos water meant incoming aircraft had little time to steady upon a target, whereas the longer approaches in the Falkland Sound gave aircraft sufficient time to attack the frigates and destroyers on the 'gun line'.

The Argentine Air Force came back on the 23rd after a day's respite, and in a welter of AA fire lost 7 or 8 jets. However, HMS **Antelope** exploded that night after the air attacks and the dramatic explosion of her magazines lit up the sky and seashore around San Carlos Water. She had been hit earlier and an unexploded bomb in her engine room detonated while being defused.

The forces ashore were now 40, 42 and 45 Commando, 2 and 3 Para with a Brigade HQ. Support arms including the medical unit which had taken over a disused refrigeration plant at Ajax Bay. For the next few days the major task was to be offloading stores and ammunition. The loss of **Atlantic Conveyor** changed many plans—with her went a large quantity of stores, and 3 vital Chinook and 6 Wessex helicopters—their spares and engineer vehicles. The loss of these helicopters was keenly felt, particularly by the Royal Marines and 3 Para who were now destined to make their epic 'yomp' across the northern route towards Stanley rather than fly.

Orders to move out from San Carlos were issued on May 26. Hardly a breakout, since the Argentine forces had not pressed the beachhead. 2 Para were to move to Camilla Creek House on the 27th and attack Goose Green and Darwin the next day. Enemy strength was reported to be around 500 men—an Infantry Company with air force personnel. 3 Para would move to Teal Inlet and 45 Commando to Douglas Settlement. 42 Commando was in reserve and 40 Commando covered the beachhead.

In an air attack on the 27th the hospital and ammunition dump at Ajax Bay was hit. Mortar bombs, missiles and artillery shells exploded all that night.

Argentine observation posts on the high ground overlooking 2 Para's route reported their likely objective and General Menendez, the Argentine Commander, helicoptered reserves from Mount Kent to Goose Green and Darwin. Suddenly the garrison there was reinforced by 1400 troops.

The battle for Goose Green lasted all day and was fought over open ground against an enemy withdrawing through fixed positions. The Paras were supported by three 105 mm guns of 8 Battery, 29 Commando Regiment RA.

A proud moment—the first Union flag is once again hauled up on the Falklands Islands by Royal Marines of 40 Commando.

The Argentine position also had three 105 mm guns and mortars, four 20 mm and 30 mm AA guns—operating in a ground role. Darwin was taken by mid morning, Goose Green airfield by the afternoon, the settlement was taken at last light. The surrender followed next morning.

Colonel H. Jones, Commanding Officer of the Battalion, was killed attacking a line of heavily defended trenches with men of his HQ Company. He was a man who believed in the best traditions of the Parachute Regiment—and led from the front.

The Paras discovered after the battle that they had fought with the odds of two to one against them. They had lost 13 killed and 34 wounded. Among the dead were the helicopter crew of a Scout helicopter piloted by Lt. Dick Nunn RM—flying on a mercy mission. Blowpipe claimed its first "kill" when a detachment from 43 AD Battery downed a Pucara. The Argentine forces lost 250 killed during the action.

On May 30th 45 Commando arrived at Douglas Settlement and 3 Para at Teal Inlet. They crossed terrain—difficult enough in good weather—through hail and rain squalls. The injury to legs and ankles were considerable since the going was either rock, marsh or rough highland grassland. The men carried their own kit as well as weapons and ammunition. This was proper 'yomping'—with about 120 lbs on each man's back. On the same day General Jeremy Moore, Commander Land Forces arrived in San Carlos as did 5 Infantry Brigade who had been rushed south.

A day later K Company 42 Commando was air lifted onto Mount Kent. It had already been well reconnoitred by an SAS squadron who harrassed the garrison and established that it was small. The Royal Marines were reinforced by two 81 mm mortars and three 105 mm guns. Meanwhile 3 Para moved from Tal Inlet to Estancia House and then to high ground nearby. The rest of 42 Cdo reinforced K Company as they consolidated on Mount Kent and Mount Challenger. The two Scorpions and four Scimitars who had followed the northern route moved south east towards Kent and Challenger.

With the Marines and Paras on Kent and Challenger, a busy time followed moving Prisoners of War back from Goose Green—and men and equipment of 5 Brigade forward. One priority was to bring the guns of 29 Cdo Regiment RA forward—with 1000 rounds per gun.

Troop Movement was by air or Landing Ship of the Royal Fleet Auxiliary. The long winter nights gave cover, not only against air attack but also against observation. One June 4 R.F.A. **Sir Tristram** and **HMS Intrepid,** with her landing craft, took Scots Guards around Bluff Cove. These landings at Fitzroy/Bluff Cove became possible after Brigadier Tony Wilson, Commander of 5 Brigade, made a public telephone call to Reg Binney the farm manager at Fitzroy to discover there were no Argentinians there.

8

Wherever British troops met Falklanders they received a terrific welcome. Here a Para is greeted with smiles and a welcome cup of tea!

Young Falkland islanders do their bit to help the Commandos establish defensive positions.

Rolls of portable road are pictured here being unloaded from a Landing Craft at Ajax Bay. The terrain at the Brigade Maintenance Area in Ajax Bay, as in most other places in the Falkland Islands, was boggy. To enable lorries and forklift trucks to move endless loads of stores, temporary roads had to be laid.

The HQ Staff of 3 Commando Brigade come ashore with their boots dry on a BARV (Beach Armoured Recovery Vehicle).

Gurkhas took over at Goose Green from 2 Para who had by now come under the command of 5 Brigade. From here they made a succession of airborne attacks against those Argentine positions still intact—but behind the forward edge of the battle area in Lafonia, the southern part of East Falkland.

As men and ammunition were moved by sea or air ever nearer Stanley, patrols went out nightly to dominate no-mans-land and examine minefields and local defences.

Back at Port San Carlos a Harrier strip had been completed and aircraft from it were called in against 155 mm guns shelling 3 Commando Brigade positions. Late in the afternoon of June 8, the two Landing Ships **Sir Tristram** and **Sir Galahad** were attacked by Skyhawks. Though Sir Tristram had almost completed off-loading, **Sir Galahad** still had a large number of Welsh Guardsmen aboard. In the fires which followed there were 146 casualties—with 63 dead. It was a very black day . . . Later Argentine A4 aircraft sank a small landing craft from HMS Fearless and a further six men were lost.

On June 10 Brigadier Julian Thompson gave orders for the capture of Mount Longdon, Two Sisters, Mount Harriet and Goat Ridge. Many of these features are similar to Dartmoor—outcrops of rocks at the top of long exposed hillsides. Some hills being linked by saddles of high ground. The men destined for this action would be from 42 Commando, 45 Commando, 3 Para with One Welsh Guards Company and two Companies of 40 Commando. 2 Para were in support. The attack was to be at night, and silent. There would be no artillery barrage.

There were two phases. First, 3 Para were to assault and capture Mount Longdon and then 42 Commando were to assault and capture Two Sisters. The Welsh Guards with the 2 Companies of 40 Commando would secure the start line for 42 Commando and then be in reserve. 2 Para was to support 3 Para.

Fire support on call was considerable, 29 Commando Regiment with 5 Batteries (two from 5 Brigade) and four RN ships. HMS **Avenger** supporting 3 Paras, HMS **Glamorgan** with 45 Commando, HMS **Yarmouth** with 42 Commando and HMS **Arrow** supporting the SAS squadron on the Murrel Hills to the north. They were given a list of 47 targets and during the subsequent fighting 3,000 rounds were fired. 3 Para fought a fierce action with the Argentine 7 Regiment who had dug themselves in amongst the crags, and used snipers. The Parachute Regiment were to suffer 14 killed and 35 wounded from their ranks. 45 Commando were faced by a strong company of 4 Regiment who used heavy macine guns effectively in the crags—they were to lose four men and 8 were wounded during the action.

42 Commando took on the remainder of 4 Regiment on Mount Harriet. The Welsh Guards Recce Platoon made a diversionary attack against the east side of the feature using Milan anti-tank missiles—while the remainder of the Commando marched around the south of the hill to attack from the east. The Argentine forces were taken by surprise, but the Royal Marines lost one man killed and a further 13 wounded. While giving naval gunfire support HMS **Glamorgan** was hit by a land-based Exocet missile and 13 men were killed. During these attacks some Argentine soldiers came forward to surrender from adjoining positions even though not under direct attack themselves. The sight of incoming fire coupled with poor motivation and leadership by their officers and NCOs made many conscripts happier to risk surrender—than death or maiming.

On the morning of the 12th gunners of 29 Commando Regiment RA, had the satisfaction of shelling an Argentine Hercules as it came in to land at Stanley—it took off promptly.

The next stage was for 2 Para to attack Wireless Ridge and 2 Scots Guards to attack Mount Tumbledown with the Gurkhas going for Mount William. During the 12th artillery fire was exchanged with 105 mm and 155 mm guns around Stanley. At night a dozen helicopters brought forward over 400 rounds of ammunition—per gun. Some guns were down to just eight rounds and re-supply was obviously critical.

In the early hours of June 14, 2 Scots Guards mounted a diversionary attack on an enemy position just south of their main objective on Tumbledown, slotting in with a move to outflank the position and move towards Stanley. This attack was part of a Brigade plan including attacks on Mount William and Sapper Hill by 1/7 Gurkha Rifles and Welsh Guards. The Scots Guards had the guns of 4th Field Regiment, and 7 (Commando) Battery on call. Once they had started firing they were to continue for the next 14 hours. Three mortar platoons and a 0.5″ machine gun platoon were also in support.

During one stage of this action the Guardsmen made a very effective but seemingly out of date assault—with fixed bayonets. The fighting was severe with Argentine Marines sticking to their positions even when wounded. The Scots Guards took 27 prisoners including the Commanding Officer of the Marines. However they lost 9 men and a further 41 were wounded. Enemy casualties were around 100.

The Gurkhas were tasked to move around the northern flank of Tumbledown when secured. As they advanced they came under artillery fire and suffered 10 casualties. Their troubles were also increased by a minefield extending northwards from Tumbledown. By great good fortune they slipped past its southern boundary.

Meanwhile the Welsh Guards were moving forward in the south. They ran into a minefield and two soldiers had their feet blown off. It was slow work—feeling a way forward through a minefield—and in the dark! The Sergeant assistant to the Battery Commander attached to the Welsh Guards, said afterwards he had never followed so closely in his leaders footsteps!

On the night of the 13th, 2 Para attacked Wireless Ridge with artillery, naval gunfire and the Blues and Royals all firing in direct support. The rapid fire cannon of their Scimitars was devastating. The weather deteriorated with howling winds, snow and sleet.

The Gurkhas reached Mount William, and the Paras were on Wireless Ridge by dawn. They could see Argentine conscripts leaving their trenches and streaming back into Stanley. It was all but over . . .

At this stage Major General Jeremy Moore used his discretion and was able to call off a cluster bomb attack against Sapper Hill with the Harriers already airborne. No doubt many lives were saved. A Spanish speaking Royal Marines Officer (Captain Rod Bell RM) made contact with the enemy by transmitting over the island's medical radio circuit. His message was:

"We wish to discuss saving lives . . . We believe a meeting should take place or a link kept open between the two opposing forces. If you fail to respond to this message and there is unnecessary bloodshed in Port Stanley, the world will judge you accordingly."

The word was passed by a civilian doctor in Stanley and after General Menendez had spoken over the radio, white flags appeared in the town.

2 Para, who had moved off Wireless Ridge as far as the island race course, paused to allow the men of 42 Commando to move through their positions into the town. It was not long before a Falklands Island flag was back on the mast at Government House.

Under the Union Flag, Royal Marines dig in at Ajax Bay.

Two Paras at Port San Carlos are ready to give any approaching enemy a "firepower demonstration".

A welcome sight to anyone who endured the Argentine air attacks in San Carlos Water—a Rapier unit. After the war the Rapier batteries were credited with 13 enemy aircraft downed.

A British soldier inspects an officer's sword left behind in the debris after Argentine troops fled a settlement near San Carlos Water.

An Argentinian Mirage makes a low level attack over the LSL Sir Bedivere. Seconds later it was shot down as it flew over the rest of the Amphibious Task Force.

# BOMB ALLEY . . .

It is no secret that the planning staffs underestimated the ferocity of the Argentine air attacks upon the amphibious force anchored in San Carlos Water.

A Pucara flew a recce mission there an hour or so after first light on the day of the landings no doubt to investigate radio reports of attack from the Argentine company on nearby Fanning Head. This first enemy aircraft met a barrage of fire, Seacat and Blowpipe missiles, Naval 4.5 inch, Bofor and Oerlikon guns, machine gun and small arms fire.

This first mission was followed, within two hours, by a succession of Mirage and Skyhawk sorties—the longest raid by 16 aircraft. But all day the bombers pressed home their attacks with incredible bravery—flying at ship's funnel height and through a curtain of fire. This bravery tended to work against them as they dropped their bombs too close to the target and many failed to explode. As time passed the air defences around San Carlos improved, in particular Rapier batteries were set up and soon became highly effective. "Bomb Alley" as San Carlos was nicknamed by the troops, became the Valley of the Shadow of Death for the Argentine pilots. They lost six out of every 10 aircraft sent to bomb the landings. Much of the air defence was provided by Sea Harriers flying combat air patrols—intercepting the Argentine aircraft on their way in towards the anchorage.

The raids did take their toll however . . . Mercifully the Argentine Air Force did not concentrate their fire power upon the shipping carrying troops and equipment—but on the warships. Wave after wave overwhelmed HMS Ardent which was with other ships providing a line of air and surface defence in the Falkland Sound. They also hit and damaged HMS Argonaut and HMS Antrim on Friday 21 May, that first day after the landing.

Two days later they repeated their wave attacks—this time HMS Antelope in the Falkland Sound was the target. She was just able to steam back into San Carlos with holes in her hull—and her main mast bent over. A Skyhawk had struck the mast before plunging into the sea, but its bomb had penetrated the frigate's engine room. A bomb disposal expert tried to defuse the 1000 pounder but it exploded soon after dusk. A fire raged deep in her hull all night. The following morning she broke her back and sank in one great cloud of steam.

Gradually Argentine losses built up and the raids slackened, nevertheless a constant vigilance was maintained on board all the ships anchored in San Carlos Water.

May 21st D Day—Landing in San Carlos Water

| Escorts | Landing Ships |
|---|---|
| HMS Broadsword | HMS Fearless |
| HMS Brilliant | HMS Intrepid |
| HMS Ardent | RFA Sir Percivale |
| HMS Argonaut | RFA Sir Tristram |
| HMS Antrim | RFA Sir Geraint |
| HMS Yarmouth | RFA Sir Galahad |
| HMS Plymouth | RFA Sir Lancelot |
| | RFA Fort Austin |
| | RFA Stromness |
| | SS Canberra |
| | M/V Norland |

Extra air defences in HMS Fearless—ad hoc but effective. This particular machine gunner put a stream of lead into the belly of a Skyhawk which crashed into San Carlos Water. It was also hit by other gunfire and, milli-seconds after the pilot ejected, by a Rapier Missile! The pilot was picked up with a badly damaged knee.

A 1000 pound bomb explodes between RFA Resource and RFA Stromness. Resource was full of ammunition and Stromness carried a further 200 tons in her forward hold!

Evening at San Carlos—an approaching pilot's view.

They came in at bridge height!—as can be seen by this Mirage. Too close to HMS Fearless for comfort.

MV Norland is straddled by bombs during a raid in San Carlos Water.

18

HMS Argonaut in San Carlos Water, severely damaged by Argentine bombs. She was unable to move—but could still fight! Day by day she licked her wounds and eventually was able to leave for further repairs—and the long journey home.

The bomb in HMS Antelope's engine room explodes, lighting up the night sky.

**SCORPION**

Scorpions and Scimitars manned by the Blues and Royals accompanied 3 Commando Brigade. They were placed in the front of the landing craft to give immediate firepower against any enemy resistance on the beaches. Later they accompanied the Royal Marines on the northern route via Douglas and Teal after the breakout from San Carlos. They survived hard terrain and bogs . . . a tribute to their designers.

**SCIMITAR**

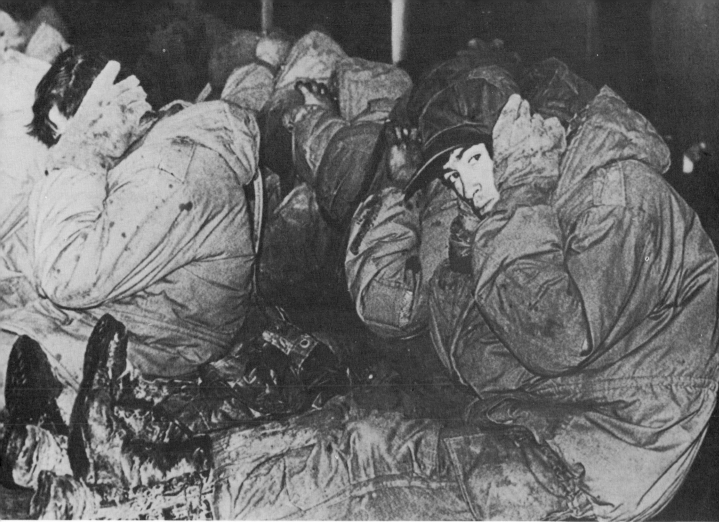

Waiting to be processed, searched and examined medically—according to the Geneva Convention—these pathetically young Argentine conscripts wait on board RFA Sir Percivale. This ship was used as an emergency shelter after an unexpectedly larger number of PoWs were taken at Goose Green.

One of the first Argentinian prisoners taken at San Carlos. He was a Lt Cdr in the Argentine Marines who had been in an observation post overlooking San Carlos Water.

Among the first PoWs were these Argentine soldiers who had been based at Fanning Head on the northern entrance to San Carlos Water. The war for them was soon over—unlike many of their former colleagues they were certain of hot meals and shelter.

The PoW camp next to the hospital at Ajax Bay—most of these prisoners were taken at Goose Green.

Marines machinery and stores are landed in quantity on the bridgehead at Ajax Bay from a Mexifloat and an LCU.

Pallet loads of ammunition boxes dominated the beach at Ajax Bay.

# FALKLAND ISLANDS

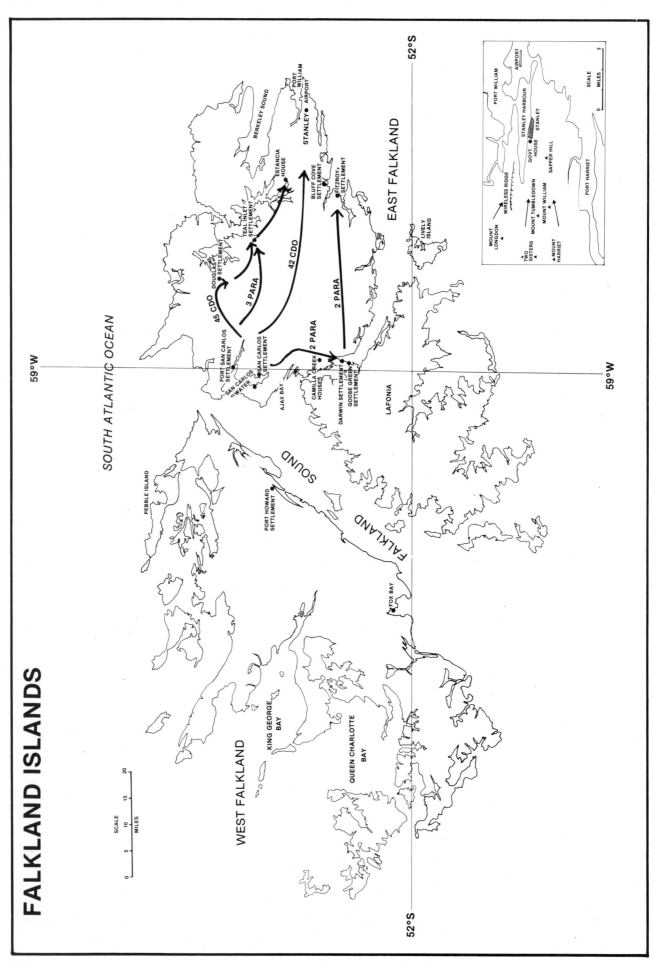

SOUTH ATLANTIC OCEAN

59°W

52°S

WEST FALKLAND

KING GEORGE BAY

QUEEN CHARLOTTE BAY

PEBBLE ISLAND

PORT HOWARD SETTLEMENT

FOX BAY

FALKLAND SOUND

EAST FALKLAND

LAFONIA

LIVELY ISLAND

BERKELEY SOUND

PORT WILLIAM

STANLEY
AIRPORT

ESTANCIA HOUSE

TEAL INLET SETTLEMENT

DOUGLAS SETTLEMENT

45 CDO

3 PARA

42 CDO

2 PARA

BLUFF COVE SETTLEMENT

FITZROY SETTLEMENT

PORT SAN CARLOS SETTLEMENT

SAN CARLOS SETTLEMENT

SAN CARLOS WATER

AJAX BAY

CAMILLA CREEK HOUSE

2 PARA

DARWIN SETTLEMENT

GOOSE GREEN SETTLEMENT

52°S

59°W

SCALE

0  5  10  15  20

MILES

MOUNT LONGDON

WIRELESS RIDGE

PORT WILLIAM

AIRPORT

STANLEY HARBOUR

GOVT. HOUSE

STANLEY

TWO SISTERS

MOUNT TUMBLEDOWN

MOUNT WILLIAM

SAPPER HILL

MOUNT HARRIET

PORT HARRIET

SCALE

0                    3

MILES

# RED AND GREEN
# LIFE SUPPORT MACHINE

Medical support to the Falkland operation was tri-service, totally integrated and very successful. Afloat, each RN ship carried a naval medical officer as part of its wartime complement, and in addition, most of the civilian ships such as the tankers and bulk freight carriers were given 'dark blue' (Royal Naval) medical staff. The luxury liner SS Canberra was rapidly converted at Southampton into a troopship with a floating hospital facility. The specialist medical staff embarked included surgeons and anaesthetists as well as the P & O medical and nursing staff who all become part of the team. Canberra's main trooping role prevented her gaining hospital ship status under the Geneva Convention like her older sister, the schools cruise ship SS Uganda. The latter underwent conversion at the Gibraltar Dockyard into the floating equivalent of a 300 bed hospital.

Each Commando unit, or infantry battalion ashore also had its integrated medical staff including two medical officers for wartime operations. For Army units such as the Parachute Regiment, or the Guards and Gurkhas, these men came from the Royal Army Medical Corps (RAMC). Royal Marines Commando units took their green-bereted medics from the Royal Naval Medical Service. When 3 Commando Brigade landed at San Carlos another group went ashore with them—the Medical Squadron of the Plymouth based Commando Logistics Regiment. Over 100 strong, this organisation is fully Arctic trained. Supporting it were two surgical teams, one from the Royal Naval Hospital at Plymouth; and the other, the Parachute Clearing Troop, from Aldershot. They were soon in action and by 31 May had completed a total of 107 major operations in the disused refrigeration plant at Ajax Bay. Although bombed and strafed by Argentinian planes attacking logistic supplies stored around the building the teams never faltered. Every British soldier who reached the facility alive went out alive, thanks to skilled surgery and stored fresh blood taken from the troops before landing.

Ajax Bay became known as the "Red and Green Life Support Machine".

A little later, 16 Field Ambulance RAMC landed at Fitzroy with 5 Infantry Brigade. They were heavily involved in the aftermath of Sir Galahad's bombing, both in coping with their own casualties (their Second in Command was among those killed) and the other injured—despite losing much of their kit. However they, with surgical teams from No. 2 Field Hospital RAMC, were soon back in business and treated many of the wounded from the final assault on Port Stanley.

Every injured man, whether treated initially at Teal Inlet, Ajax Bay or Fitzroy, was flown to the Uganda. There wounds were reassessed before patients were declared fit for onward evacuation by hospital transport ships (the converted survey vessels HMS Hydra, Hecla and Hecate) to Montevideo in Uruguay. The long arm of the RAF stretched to Montivideo and gathered the casualties into VC10s for a comfortable jet borne flight back to England.

The death toll was high enough—255 men of the Task Force died and 777 were injured. But thanks to efficient first aid, and high quality medical treatment along the evacuation chain, only three men died of their wounds. This is a remarkable figure and perfect testimony to the dedication and skill of the medical men and women who all played their part in achieving it.

Not exactly Harley Street . . .
The abandoned refrigeration plant at Ajax Bay became the field hospital. Many men of the Force owe their lives to the skill of the medical men who operated on them in appalling conditions in these tin sheds.

The naval medical assistant of J Company 42 Commando gives first aid to wounded Argentine PoWs on Mount Harriet. This medic had been with the small Royal Marines detachment in Stanley when the Argentinians invaded.

A first aid party on board HMS Fearless tends an Argentine pilot after he had been shot down over San Carlos Water.

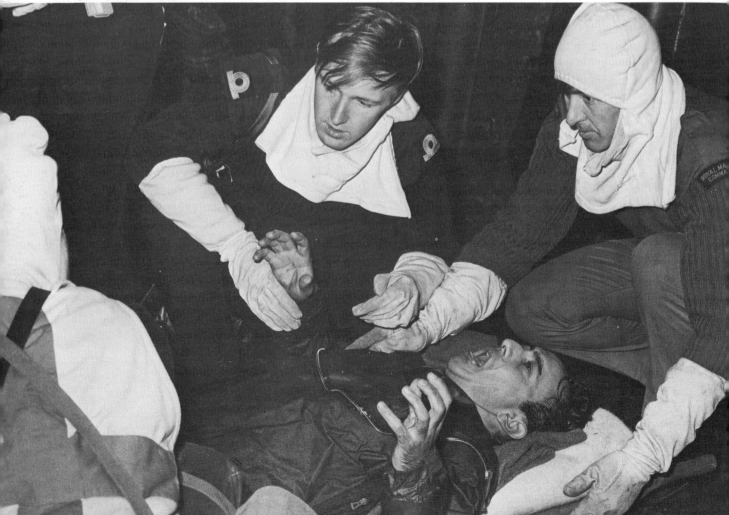

A Royal Marines medical team patch up a wounded Argentine soldier and prepare him for the helicopter ride to the hospital at Ajax Bay.

All types of helicopters, including Scouts and Gazelles were used for casualty evacuation. A Bluff Cove casualty is pictured here being carried to the hospital having been flown in from the battlefield.

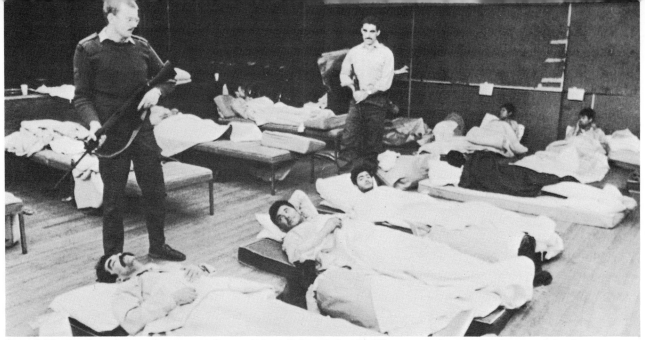

Royal Marine bandsmen keep guard over injured Argentine PoWs recovering in the hospital facility on board SS Canberra.

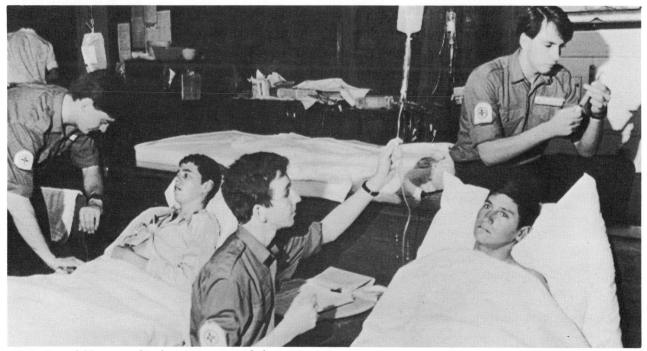

While Royal Navy medical assistants tend their injuries.

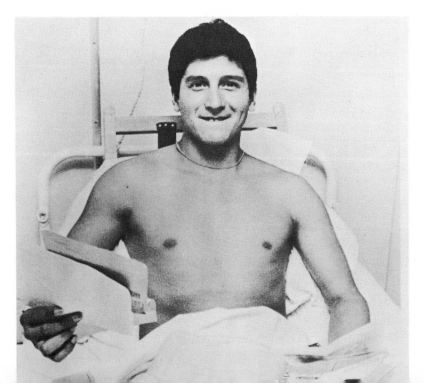

Argentine PoW Miguel Garcia's picture appeared in many UK and foreign newspapers after he had been taken on board Canberra suffering from gunshot wounds. He is seen here with some of the many letters he received from Britain wishing him a speedy recovery—humanity triumphing over war!

After the Battle for Goose Green . . .

The reality of war—Major General Moore (centre) and many of his troops pay their last respects to comrades killed in the Goose Green battle.

An RAF intelligence officer examines stocks of Argentine napalm bombs discovered at Goose Green airstrip after the Argentines had surrendered.

The survivors of the attack on LSL Sir Galahad. She was hit in a Skyhawk raid before she had disembarked her Welsh Guard passengers. Apparently the stern ramp was down and a bomb was flung through it onto the ship's main tank deck.

Clouds of black smoke hampered helicopter crews rescuing survivors. But again and again they flew blind—through choking clouds—regardless of the obvious danger to themselves to pluck men out of the icy waters. Helicopter pilots even used the downwash of their rotors to blow rescue rafts away from the inferno.

Firefighting on the Royal Fleet Auxiliary logistic ship Sir Galahad ten days after the bomb attack—it took that long to extinguish the flames.

An "Eager-Beaver" fork lift truck of the Commando Logistics Regiment gets stuck in the ever-present mud while unloading stores at Teal Inlet.

Air Defence Troop, 3 Commando Brigade dig in at Teal Inlet . . . in the fog.

Much welcome help from a local farmer at Teal Inlet.

Warrant Officer Pat Chapman, RSM of 45 Commando leads the "yomp" out of Teal Inlet eastwards to the mountains and . . . eventually Stanley.

**Mortar Troop 42 Commando about to be airlifted by Wessex helicopter onto Mount Kent.**

**K Company, 42 Commando move into commanding positions on Mount Kent.**

A naval photographer in action! Petty Officer Peter Holgate put his camera down during a tense moment on Mount Kent.

Meanwhile . . . back at home wives and families could only watch and wait—glued to the TV and Radio for news of their menfolk.

Bombardment by the 105 mm guns of 7 Battery, 29 Commando Regiment, Royal Artillery.

The old soldier's maxim—"Whenever possible—brew up!"

After eight days on Mount Challenger K Company 42 Commando move forward to their next objective.

Marines of 45 Commando trudge past Mount Tumbledown on their way into Stanley, with over snow vehicles carrying some of their heavier kit. These vehicles were, with the Scorpions and Scimitars, the only vehicles which could cope with the alternating bogs and rocky terrain of East Falkland.

Commandos pick their way through a minefield a few miles west of Stanley.

At the end of the epic yomp . . . J Company of 42 Commando marching on the road between the old Marine Barracks at Moody Brook and Stanley. J Company was an ad hoc company formed on board SS Canberra from Naval Party 8901 — the troops who had fought the Argentines during their invasion — and 42 Commando's Defence and Milan Troops. It was commanded by Major Mike Norman who had commanded NP 8901.

A 105 mm light gun of 79 Battery, 29 Commando Regiment, Royal Artillery about to fire at Argentinian positions from its position at Estancia House.

Naval gunfire support during the final advance upon Stanley.

## The Falklands Conflict—as reported by the Royal Navy's own South Atlantic Patrol Vessel HMS ENDURANCE

HMS Endurance.

ENDURANCE's last Antarctic season was coming to a close as the red ship returned to Stanley on the 19 March 1982, back from work on the west side of the Antarctic Peninsula. Perhaps it was with feelings of relief that the major slice of the deployment was over and that the ship's company could look forward to the programmed pleasures of visits to Buenos Aires, Barbados, Azores and then the delights of getting home on the 20 May. Well, that was the plan . . .

The stay in Stanley for the ship's company was only to be a short one, ENDURANCE was tasked to take passage to Montevideo and then return with the new Royal Marines for Naval Party 8901. The ship's Flight and ENDURANCE Marines, were to be disembarked during the Montevideo journey and undertake an extensive period of training on the hills of the Falklands. All these plans came to nothing, the ship was sent to South Georgia following the landing on the island of Mr. Davidoff's scrap men who began to dismantle the old whaling station of Leith. HMS ENDURANCE then left South Georgia, at the end of March, to sail in protection of the Falklands when events there were obviously deteriorating. She left Grytviken hugging the coast hoping to escape unnoticed by the patrolling Argentine ice breaker lurking outside the harbour. She was successful. A Royal Marine Party had, however, been put ashore to protect the island base at Grytviken under the command of Lt Keith Mills RM.

ENDURANCE's journey into the fresh westerly swell of the southern ocean was uncomfortable and slow, and she did not expect to arrive at Stanley until the morning of 4 April 1982. The ship worked on establishing suitable communications links with Grytviken, but was keen to prevent any demands to establish radio links that would disclose her position. Preparations included spraying the helicopters to camouflage them against the Falkland Hills.

## The Falkland Invasion . . .

The initial attack on the Falklands came at 0430 local time when commandos went ashore in the vicinity of Mullet Creek. The main assault, an hour and a half later, followed in Yorke Bay and the personnel carriers moved along the airport road to Port Stanley. The leading vehicle was struck by a Carl Gustav missile and the crews of the remaining vehicles disembarked. Lieutenant Richard Ball was maintaining guard of the local Argentines in the Town Hall, whilst the rest of the survey team operated an information service in Government House before assisting in the final defence of the building.

This survey party were finishing the survey of Berkeley Sound. During the run up to the invasion they were called in to help the local Royal Marines defend the town of Stanley. All were taken prisoner and returned to the UK. Most of their hydrographic results were either lost to the Argentines or put in the attics of a few local houses for safe custody!

Endurance found out that the invasion was complete when the British Antarctic Base at Signy spoke to Grytviken. It was learned that no civilian casualties had occurred, although some Argentines were in hospital. After the invasion had taken place ENDURANCE was ordered to retrace her tracks to South Georgia, and if possible support her military "garrison" there. With reports that all was now quiet in Port Stanley, ENDURANCE began to make plans for dealing with any enemy action at Grytviken.

## The Defence of Grytviken

After a fairly quiet start to their defence of the new garrison at Grytviken, the Royal Marines—after hearing the news of the Argentine invasion of the Falkland Islands—set about preparing their defences. The beaches were wired with some home-made weapons, and a plan was laid to secure their withdrawal to the mountains by escaping through the gap towards Maiviken. Rucksacks with stores and ammunition were placed along the trail. The British Antarctic scientists took refuge in the unique whaling station church, leaving the base commander behind—to help with radio communications.

The Marines had placed two men on Jason ridge to observe activities, but with the high sea state it was not possible to recover them until the following morning. ENDURANCE made contact with the Garrison in code, informing the RM Commander that she would be in the vicinity to help at 1500 the next day, 3 April. The two men on surveillance duties were collected from Jason Ridge. It was learned from them that the PARAISO was at anchor in Leith and an Argentine corvette was heading into Stromness Bay . . . At 1030 the PARAISO made radio contact with the Royal Marines. ENDURANCE was able to listen in to one side of the conversation. The message was clear:

> "Following our successful operation in the Malvinas Islands the ex-governor has surrendered the islands and dependencies to Argentina. We suggest you adopt a similar course of action to prevent any further loss of life."

In an attempt to gain some time, Lieutenant Keith Mills asked for amplification and clarification, reading back the message on HF to ensure ENDURANCE knew what was going on. He further asked for time to consider the PARAISO's request. He was given five minutes! PARAISO came back by radio asking all personnel on the base to assemble on the beach so they could be counted from seaward. As the message came in the Argentine corvette GUERRICO rounded the point and headed into the cove, and a helicopter flew overhead. The PARAISO was then informed there was a British military presence and any attempt to land would be repulsed. The Base Commander withdrew to the civilian sanctuary of the Norwegian whaling church, and Lieutenant Mills moved down towards the jetty at King Edward Point, to commence negotiations with the Argentine boat party, which he assumed would arrive. At the same time the corvette headed back out into East Cumberland Bay and he was somewhat surprised by an Argentine helicopter disgorging seven marines nearby. A Puma helicopter from the PARAISO then attempted to land on the foreshore—as a volley of fire from the machine guns set up by invading Argentines on the opposite side of the cove, engaged the British defensive positions. The order was given to fire on the Puma. About five hundred rounds were pumped at the helicopter, which, remarkably, was still able to fly. With some excellent airmanship on the part of the pilot it covered the 400 metres to the other side of the cove. The aircraft trailed smoke to the site, where it made a very heavy landing. No one was seen to climb out. Two months later, the Puma still lay on its side where it had landed.

An Alouette helicopter making further troop reinforcements on the opposite side of the cove, was engaged with gunfire causing it to drop out of the sky severely damaged. The corvette GUERRICO then began to re-enter the cove to support the landing, firing her 40 mm after gun. To the surprise, and delight, of the Royal Marines, the ship steamed on her slow relentless course, and when only about 300 metres from the base the Marines fired one 84 mm Carl Gustav, which dived into the water 10 metres short of the ship, and struck the starboard quarter below the water line. It exploded. The ship's forward 100 mm turret was damaged by 66 mm and heavy machine gunfire. As the corvette came increasingly under fire, she turned and retraced her tracks into the safety of the bay. The battering did not stop, however, and anti-tank rockets struck her Exocet launchers. (The Argentines disclosed later that 1275 hits were scored on the GUERRICO. No information of any casualties was given.) Having reached the bay she turned and began shelling the area from a range of 3000 metres using her damaged 100 mm gun for about 20 minutes. By this time the Argentine Marines had moved around the cove through the whaling station, and had cut off the Royals

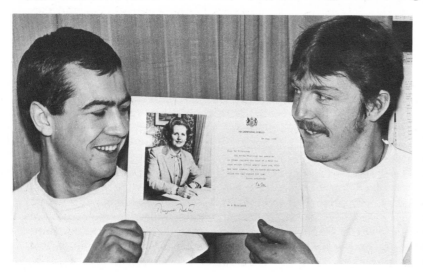

Getting somewhat bored onboard Endurance during the war the lads of 4 mess decided to drop the Prime Minister a line complementing her on her handling of the situation. They also said they though her a "snazzy dresser"! Much to their surprise back came a photo from the boss—proudly displayed by Cooks "Ginge" Doogan and Robby Wilkinson.

proposed route of withdrawal. With one casualty amongst his men the Royal Marine Commander quickly reassessed his position and decided that the point at issue had been made—military force had been used to take the island, and little was to be gained by a suicidal defence. Without a surrender flag available, a make-shift flag in the shape of a coat was held aloft and the shooting stopped. The two Commanding Officers met to negotiate the surrender, and the 22 Royal Marines put down their arms. The civilian scientists were released from their refuge, the most southerly church in the world, and the prisoners were taken on board the BAHIA PARAISO. Eleven days later they were disembarked at Puerto Belgrano—and housed in a swimming pool at the base.

The Marines returned to England on the 20 April via Montevideo. As a result of this brave defence by 22 men against 100 marines, 3 helicopters and 2 ships, the Commanding Officer Lieutenant Keith Mills and his Second-in-Command Sgt Peter Leach were awarded the DSC and DSM respectively. HMS ENDURANCE was unable to help the Royal Marines because although she had been steaming hard she was too far away. During the mid-afternoon of the same day, when the ship was at the extreme range for a recce flight, a Wasp helicopter, fully camouflaged in its new colours was launched. It landed in the cover of the mountains. The pilot, Lieutenant Commander Tony Ellerbeck and Observer, Lieutenant David Wells, climbed to a high point leaving the Wasp obscured by the hill. They watched GUERRICO slowly moving but labouring after the damage inflicted. PARAISO was hidden from view, but supporting landing craft were seen moving into King Edwards Point Jetty. A helicopter was operating to the shore. There were no signs of the Royal Marine detachment—they were assumed to be held on board one of the ships. ENDURANCE was required to remain in her covert role using the cover of the bays, coves and icebergs along the coast of the island, which necessitated operating in areas which had never been charted. At night she resorted to immitating an iceberg amongst the north going bergs in order to hide from enemy radar. HMS ENDURANCE was the only British warship in the southern hemisphere and was likely to remain so for at least another week. Back in the UK the task force was just being assembled.

For ENDURANCE a major offensive was out of the question, and she was advised by the Commander-in-Chief to remain covert, watch proceedings, and use her local knowledge to best advantage. Even though the Argentines had cleared Grytviken of its British population there were a number of other civilians in less accessible places. As it transpired all these people remained secure from Argentine forces until the island was recaptured. They had to sit it out for three weeks.

The nature of ENDURANCE's activities at this time produced much press interest. The Ministry of Defence and all in ENDURANCE were keen to ensure that nothing provoked the Argentines to mount any further offensive against the ship. The Argentine propaganda machine had even helped in this. An announcement was made in the Argentine press that ENDURANCE had been sunk. This news was given coverage at home, and it obviously gave families and friends at home an anxious few days. The Government decided late on the 4 April, just 36 hours after the taking of Grytviken to sail ENDURANCE north to unite her with the southbound ships of the task force. Hearts lifted as the ship left the protection of the icebergs and made her way north into warmer waters.

## The Force assembles in the Southern Hemisphere

On 12 April the ENDURANCE rendezvoused with RFA FORT AUSTIN and a number of troops were embarked. ENDURANCE, extremely low on food, undertook a massive replenishment, but was saddened to see their first load of lamb chops fall into the sea when a Wessex helicopter suffered engine failure. Two days later the ship saw her first British warship for 6 months when HMS ANTRIM and HMS PLYMOUTH arrived to complete the small task unit to recapture South Georgia. HMS ANTRIM and HMS PLYMOUTH steamed past "cheering ship", and it was a very relieved ship's company that welcomed the protection of these well armed vessels. The ship was also able to welcome back the survey team which had been captured by the Argentines in the Falklands. ENDURANCE then had to quickly relearn the business of working with other RN units. Nowhere was it tested more, than during the refuelling operation with the group's tanker TIDESPRING. It proved to be a first. There had never been a requirement in the previous deployments in the South Atlantic to refuel at sea—tanks onboard normally kept over a month's supply of fuel. The mini task force having assembled, moved south towards South Georgia and undertook a massive exchange of embarked troops around the four ships of the force. Immense quantities of ammunition, weapons and special equipment was stored to meet the hostile and unusual environment of South Georgia. Under the control of the Task Group Commander in HMS ANTRIM the force was within sight of South Georgia on the 21 April—the day before President Galtieri visited the Falklands to encourage his troops and enhance his political reputation.

Plans had already been made to insert special forces to collect information on enemy positions. Two main locations were chosen for these insertions, one at Hound Bay, and the other at Fortuna Bay with access to Fortuna Glacier.

The landing at Fortuna Glacier resulted in a number of men being trapped on the glacier—they were unable to move forward across the wildly crevassed ice. In blinding snow a rescue helicopter was deployed from RFA TIDESPRING to bring back the men; it crashed in "white out" conditions on the glacier, but all on board survived. A second rescue helicopter also crashed, some of the troops had the disturbing experience of being involved in successive aircrashes within minutes. A third helicopter from HMS ANTRIM succeeded in penetrating the weather and brought all the men back to safety. For this action the pilot received the DSC. During this period an ENDURANCE rating was taken to St. Andrew's Bay to join 3 scientists and two members of a film crew living in a hut. Previous experience by ENDURANCE proved that this precaution was necessary, since well-intended actions by the isolated Britons resulted in reports about an ENDURANCE helicopter, being given over the radio to other locations. With the RN rating at the hut, radio talk was turned to the advantage of the naval force.

## The Task Force Takes Grytviken and Leith

The night of the 24 April was spent as quietly as possible, camouflaged amongst the icebergs to the south of the island. Just before dawn, ENDURANCE moved northeast along the coast to close Grytviken, and rendezvoused with the rest of the task group. Not long after dawn a message was received that an enemy surface submarine was at the mouth of Cumberland Bay, and was being attacked by a British Wessex helicopter on patrol. ANTRIM's helicopter had conducted a surface search close to the shore, and had found the submarine on the surface. The Wessex engaged the vessel with a depth charge causing some damage. Immediately, ENDURANCE launched her Wasp with two AS12 missiles—the helicopter located the submarine and attacked the conning tower. The Wasp returned for a second load, as the second Wasp was launched. Other attacks were made from HMS BRILLIANT and HMS PLYMOUTH. As the submarine closed the harbour the helicopters came under mortar and machine gunfire from the shore. Considerable damage was done to the submarine before it came to rest alongside the jetty at King Edward Point.

As the attack on the submarine was taking place, HMS BRILLIANT joined the task group and her helicopters were launched to take part. The task group commander decided to make the most of the offensive and the Argentinian's inertia, and sustain the effort to recover the island. ANTRIM and PLYMOUTH formed up on the gun line and without risk to life at the base, bombarded the opposite shore in the cove to impress the enemy with the group's firepower. Very quickly the Argentines raised the white flag, sang their national anthem, and lowered the Argentinian flag after just 23 days of occupation at Grytviken.

HMS PLYMOUTH and HMS ENDURANCE were sent to Leith to seize the area where the scrap men had first been landed. The small garrison was called on the radio by ENDURANCE and asked to surrender. In reply the military Commander requested that the civilians be given safe refuge. They were directed to leave Leith and walk around the point to Stromness, the next whaling station. He refused however to surrender the military force.

One hour later, as darkness fell, the military Commander, who turned out to be Captain Astiz, did agree to surrender and was asked to assemble his troops on the football field—a few hundred metres to the west of Leith. This the Commander refused to do—it later transpired the football field was heavily mined including a particularly potent charge under the helicopter landing H provided. Realizing the implications of sending men into the whaling station in the dark, ENDURANCE directed Captain Astiz to remain in Leith overnight, and move out of the station at dawn to a specified hill, where the surrender would be accepted. This was a fortunate move—it transpired that it was the intention of the Argentines, to operate explosive devices had anyone entered the whaling station after the surrender. The ceremony at which Captain Astiz formally surrendered was held on board HMS PLYMOUTH. Nearly two hundred prisoners and civilian detainees were taken, in an operation with only one major injury; a seaman on board SANTA FE suffered a leg injury which subsequently required amputation.

The following day the submarine, SANTA FE, with the aid of members of the Argentine crew, was moved from King Edward Point Jetty to the whaling station. In an unfortunate incident Chief Petty Officer Artuso was killed. The submarine was later effectively immobilized to prevent its further use. Later in the week CPO Artuso was given a full military funeral and was laid to rest in the Grytviken cemetery alongside Sir Ernest Shackleton and those who have died in the port from whaling accidents.

## South Georgia Becomes a Forward Operating Base

The prisoners were finally embarked in RFA TIDESPRING and taken to Ascension Island, where all but Captain Astiz were flown home via Montevideo.

After about a week of cleaning up the debris of the Argentine invasion, all ships except ENDURANCE departed South Georgia leaving M Company 42 Royal Marines to defend the area from renewed Argentine activity. It was considered possible, although unlikely, that a few Argentines may have gone to hide in the hostile mountains; and that the Argentines may attempt some air attack on the base or ships in the area. Neither actually materialised. Britain had been able to demonstrate to the world that victory was accomplished with the minimum of force. Its diplomatic value was immense.

Military action started in the Falklands at the beginning of May, with air strikes and the torpedoing of the General Belgrano; in consequence South Georgia slid into the background of world news.

ENDURANCE's work from early May until she sailed for Southern Thule on 17 June was of considerable value to the progress of the offensive in the Falklands. In logistic terms, South Georgia's harbours became consolidation points where requisitioned merchant ships exchanged loads and passengers for onward movement to the Falkland Islands battle zone. In the absence of adequate moorings and harbour facilities, ships using the ports needed to tailor their operations to suit the weather. On a number of occasions, ships put to sea after dragging their anchor.

At Leith the ship's divers worked hard to clear a considerable quantity of explosive from the beaches and workshops at the whaling station. Eventually the place was cleared of weapons and effects, much of it was burned.

In late May the Cable Ship IRIS sailed into Grytviken harbour bringing with them the ENDURANCE Royal Marines from the UK. They had sailed from Grytviken aboard the Argentine ship BAHIA PARAISO as prisoners. By this time ships near the Falklands were suffering damage from Argentine aircraft and missiles. ENDURANCE was asked to supply steel from the old whaling station stocks. Working parties were deployed to Leith, Stromness and Husvik to recover steel plate and angle iron—all still in a remarkable state of preservation. The Cable Ship IRIS loaded these stocks for delivery to STENA SEASPREAD in the battle zone.

On 27 May, the harbour at Grytviken played host to the largest gathering of ships in its history. CANBERRA, QUEEN ELIZABETH 2, NORLAND, IRIS, HMS LEEDS CASTLE, RMAS TYPHOON, HMS FARNELLA, JUNELLA, NORTHELLA, CORDELLA and PICT, and of course ENDURANCE. It was an important phase in the war, as the near 3,000 troops on the QE2 were an essential part of the offensive plan on the Falklands. It took nearly three days to complete the transfer and get the P and O and Cunard ships under way again. The period was blessed with such low cloud that at times the funnel of the QE2 would disappear into it, and load carrying helicopters would transit invisibly with their underslung loads moving across the horizon as if carried by the proverbial "sky-hook". The cloud was a great protection from possible Argentine bombing.

On the last day the skies cleared and reports were received of high level aircraft overhead. Earlier the tanker BRITISH WYE had been bombed by a Hercules aircraft 200 miles north of South Georgia and the news was received with some gravity on board. The ships taking part in the transfer were sailed as quickly as possible to ensure their safety. The weather had generally been on our side. That night most of the ships left the area, those ships that stayed behind were located inshore or alongside. ENDURANCE sailed to Leith to protect RFA STROMNESS throughout the following day. Both Wasps were deployed to high ground, the guns were manned, and everyone stood on full alert and listened for any give-away aircraft noise. It never came and within two days the threat was deemed to have passed and ENDURANCE resumed her normal routine.

The gambit paid off. The routine was broken by news of the excellent progress being made by our forces.

The whole task force waited and wondered what the Argentine reaction would be following the fall of Stanley. As time went by it became clear that the Argentines had had enough and this particular battle was over. For ENDURANCE the operation was not yet complete however.

## The Taking of Southern Thule

In 1976, the Argentines landed on Southern Thule, the southern most of eleven islands in the South Sandwich group. The islands are volcanic—with three of them still active. The Argentines settled on Southern Thule to secure the same sovereignty rights as they demanded for the Falklands and South Georgia.

Many British diplomatic protests were made to the Argentine Government over the years—all of them were ignored. The base established was used as a communication centre and tropospheric measuring location—sited on the south east promontory of Thule Island. It was decided that the removal of the Argentines from "their" Southern Thule base was next on the agenda . . . ENDURANCE was ordered to deploy a task group to remove the unwelcome residents. It was approaching the darkest day of the year in the southern hemisphere, and the pack ice was moving rapidly northwards in its seasonal change. Each year the ice encircles the whole of the Sandwich group and satellite pictures indicated the ice front was 30 miles to the south of the island. It was thus a race against time, temperatures had already fallen to minus eight degrees Celcius and effectively a lot lower in 40 knot winds. It looked as if the weather was going to be the main problem.

ENDURANCE and the SALVAGEMAN set off from South Georgia on 17 June having declared their intentions to the Argentines at Southern Thule. They gave no undertaking to surrender. HMS YARMOUTH and RFA OLMEDA, with M Company Royal Marines followed the next day. On 19 June, ENDURANCE hiding to the north of the island began inserting M Company recce troops using an 848 Squadron Wessex. Wessex helicopters had not operated from ENDURANCE's deck before, but after trials in Cumberland Bay, South Georgia, it was found possible, not only to operate this much larger aircraft on the deck, but also to stow it in the hangar and still keep the normal complement of two Wasps in the other half.

Two Blowpipe anti-aircraft missile operators were embarked to give the ship anti-aircraft protection from possible Argentine Hercules attack. The insertion was completed successfully following the recce by an ENDURANCE Wasp in poor weather conditions. To safeguard the troop carrier the Wessex was accompanied by an AS12 missile carrying Wasp on each of the trips to the island. In the chilling minus 11 degrees C temperature and high winds, the troops began their slow climb around the exposed ice-covered terrain to the south of the island, using the low cloud as cover. An alert Argentine carrying out an inspection had spotted one of the recce party, and returned to the base to raise the alarm. The element of surprise had gone . . . By night fall it was becoming evident that the recce troops, even though they had been spotted,

Sergeant Napier leads his men into a borrowed Wessex 5 for the raid against Southern Thule.

Sub Lt. Martinez—the Base Commander at Southern Thule surrenders onboard HMS Endurance. The Commanding Officer of all the units involved witness the surrender.
L to R (Seated) C.O. Tug Salvageman, 'M' Company 40 Commando RM: HMs Endurance, HMS Yarmouth & RFA Olmeda.

Southern Thule. The Union Flag goes up again.

would have to stay on the island, and that the extreme weather conditions were going to make any airborne assault a difficult business. In the strong wind conditions the marines assessed the temperature, including the chill factor, had fallen to an incredible 35 deg C.

The plan formulated was to frighten the station staff into surrender the following morning by a sequence of naval gunfire from HMS YARMOUTH aimed at Twitcher Rock. At first light the following morning the ships took up their positions close to the shore. ENDURANCE closed to half a mile off the shore and the Argentine shore party came out on to the promontory waving a white flag. They had become less and less able to function as they had systematically smashed all radio, meteorological, domestic and other equipment at the base. It was estimated, by the Argentines, that they had inflicted three million dollars worth of damage in a two-day orgy of destruction.

On shore the recce troops swept into the base, followed by M Company troops, under the command of Captain Chris Nunn, Royal Marines, in a Seaking from RFA OLMEDA. Further marines were also taken ashore from ENDURANCE. No resistance was met, not one shot was fired, and there were no casualties incurred to recover the base for Britain. Ten prisoners, all but one military, were taken and were embarked on board the task group ships. A surrender ceremony witnessed by all the Commanding Officers, was held in the wardroom of HMS ENDURANCE.

OLMEDA and YARMOUTH returned north with the prisoners and ENDURANCE followed two days later with her ever faithful shadow—the tug SALVAGEMAN.

## One last job . . .
## Refloating the Submarine SANTE FE

On her return to South Georgia from Southern Thule, ENDURANCE set about the job of raising the submarine SANTE FE lying alongside the Grytviken whaling jetty. Previous unsuccessful attempts indicated that more resources in terms of pumps, manpower and technical expertise were required if the boat was to be raised. On 28 June, SALVAGEMAN was moored alongside the submarine, and a coffer dam was erected around the conning tower. More pumps were brought in and eventually access was gained to the all important blow panel. Lt Cdrs Ives and Ainslie directed the operation with the aid of SALVAGEMAN's expertise and the ship's divers led by Lieutenant O'Connell. This unlikely combination of Hydrographic Officer and Supply Officer bemused some of the distant observers in England. Without drawings or a personal knowledge of the submarine, the team gradually gained access to the vital compartments in the vessel. Leaks both fore and aft slowed down the operation. Access was made more difficult by the copious quantities of diesel oil within the pressure hull, together with other noxious chemicals such as battery acid and feculent residue. Working conditions were not good!!

Pumping continued day and night, only to be interrupted by occasional pump failure. The team went into watches to maintain progress, and assure no setbacks. As the water receded an array of other "nasties" were revealed. These were mainly volatile and unstable explosives and detonators, and of course the torpedoes. After the forward section rose out of the water, further access could be obtained through the forward hatch, and with extra pumps from the Cable Ship IRIS, the water receded at a fast rate. Eventually, a number of leaks both forward and aft were located and sealed, and finally on 14 July the stern lifted when another ballast tank was blown. It left the submarine buoyant, stable, but with a 20 degree list to port, leaving the conning tower leaning against the tug SALVAGEMAN. With increasing danger from the drying explosives, it was decided to move the vessel to a prearranged location near the Hestesletten in Cumberland Bay, clear of all personnel and buildings. There she remains today, a tangible sign of the war in South Georgia.

On 16 July ENDURANCE left South Georgia bound for a week's visit to the Falkland Islands and then home . . . it had been an extremely long deployment.

The tug Salvageman with the Argentinian submarine Santa Fe alongside being eased out of harbour by the tug Yorkshireman following salvage operations.

# FULL HOUSE AT SAN CARLOS

Sunset from the bridge of HMS Glamorgan—outside San Carlos Water.

# FAREWELL TO A FINE SHIP . . .

## HMS Coventry—the last half hour

Three bombs explode deep in her hull.

She comes to rest . . . her port side ripped out

# STANLEY

**At the airport**—all that remains of a Pucara.

**In Town**—damage to civilian property—
all part of the price that had to be paid.

# HOME AT LAST

**SS Canberra**—the "Great White Whale" of the South Atlantic arrives to a heroes welcome.

# HMS YARMOUTH

HMS YARMOUTH arrived off the Falklands in late April after a passage which included the normal exercises and two-day call at Ascension Island. Straight away she found herself in action and, on 1 May, with HMS BRILLIANT, she spent the whole day using her sonars, helicopter and mortars to hunt for a suspected submarine. HMS YARMOUTH formed part of the protective escort for the carriers as the group patrolled to the east of the islands enforcing the blockade. When, on 4 May, SHEFFIELD was hit by an Exocet missile, ARROW and YARMOUTH having narrowly been missed by a second missile, went to her aid. Whilst ARROW was fighting the fire, YARMOUTH fought off a possible submarine attack.

For the next four days of foggy weather YARMOUTH remained with the carrier group before being despatched to take the still floating SHEFFIELD in tow. She went alongside the stricken ship in the early hours of 9 May and passed a tow. For twenty-nine hours SHEFFIELD, with the White Ensign still flying, was towed—within range of enemy aircraft—until, as the wind increased to gale force, she heeled over and, at 7 a.m. on 10 May, sank. YARMOUTH headed back towards the Task Force.

A week of storms followed and YARMOUTH, the oldest escort ship in the Task Force, rode out the weather with no damage—despite her twenty-two years. On 19 May the amphibious landing group arrived, joined the Task Force and headed West to the Falkland Sound. During the landing YARMOUTH's task was to provide anti-submarine and anti-air protection. Throughout the bright, sunny day she patrolled in Falkland Sound as enemy Mirage and A4 aircraft attacked both the landing area in San Carlos Water and the ships protecting the landing force. During one such attack in the afternoon, ARDENT was hit and set on fire. Shortly afterwards another wave of Skyhawks again attacked ARDENT—she immediately began to list and to burn fiercely. YARMOUTH went to her aid and took off the ship's company as the fire spread towards the magazines. She then headed for San Carlos Water where she transferred ARDENT's crew to SS CANBERRA before resuming her patrol in the Sound.

The next 10 days saw YARMOUTH in San Carlos Water by day—leaving at dusk each night to carry out a variety of tasks including shore bombardment, anti-submarine patrols, covert operations and escorting merchant ships to and from the landing area. Each morning at dawn she returned to San Carlos Water to provide anti-aircraft protection for the landing ships. This was a particularly testing time for the 250 men onboard as they spent the daylight hours at Action Stations, subject to frequent air attacks, and with little time for sleep at night. Many ships present at that time suffered damage from air attacks and only the concentrated fire of YARMOUTH's 4.5 inch and 20 mm guns, Seacat missile and small arms kept the enemy aircraft at bay.

After this testing period, YARMOUTH sailed east to the repair area and spent two days carrying out essential maintenance before rejoining the Task Force. Most nights during the following week (6-13 June) the ship bombarded enemy positions to the west of Port Stanley with her 4.5 inch guns. During the conflict she fired well over 1000 rounds—some thirty-two tons of shells! The ship's ageing machinery performed extremely well as YARMOUTH dashed nearly two hundred miles to and from the Islands at high speed to carry out the bombardment by night and then back to the battle group to replenish fuel and ammunition.

On one such mission the ship encountered a small coaster, packed with Gurkhas and essential supplies, immobilised by a rope around her propeller and prey for enemy aircraft. YARMOUTH's diving team freed her screws, and the vessel was able to sail to Goose Green. On another night the frigate stood by and provided firefighting and medical aid to HMS GLAMORGAN when the destroyer was hit by an Exocet.

After Port Stanley had been re-taken, YARMOUTH was despatched to South Georgia, and from there to Southern Thule to join HMS ENDURANCE to enforce the surrender of its Argentine contingent. She later took the prisoners of war from South Georgia to Port Stanley. On 7 July, after several more days patrolling with the Battle Group, she began her eight thousand mile voyage home in company with EXETER and CARDIFF. Apart from INVINCIBLE she was the last of the original Task Force to leave the area.

In the four months April to July, YARMOUTH steamed almost 40,000 miles, through fog, storms, icy seas and snow and reached almost sixty degrees south.

Many people, including those of Great Yarmouth, who adopted the ship, the workers of Rosyth Dockyard, the people of Fife and families and friends of the ship's company had every reason to feel proud of HMS YARMOUTH when she returned home in late July.

HMS Yarmouth, her hull pockmarked with cannon fire and rockets, helps HMS Fearless fight off attacks by the Argentine Air Force.

# HMS PLYMOUTH

HMS PLYMOUTH (with HMS ANTRIM and RFA TIDEPOOL) were detached ahead of the Task Force to repossess South Georgia, whilst still north of Ascension. Some 200 troops were embarked in the three ships, including Royal Marines and Special Air Service units. Lt Cdr Astiz, who commanded a section of the Argentine forces at Leith surrendered on board PLYMOUTH on Monday 26 April, other forces having surrendered at Grytviken the previous night.

The ship rejoined the main Task Force in time for the first Vulcan attacks on Stanley airfield and the retaliatory Argentinian air raids of 1 May, but was then sent north to escort the amphibious assault force, including the liner CANBERRA. In company with the amphibious ships, HMS PLYMOUTH was the first vessel to enter San Carlos Water during the night of 20/21 May, escorting waves of landing craft to the beaches. For the remainder of that day the ship took part in the air defence of the assault force from Argentinian air attack and later assisted the damaged frigate HMS ARGONAUT after she had been hit. PLYMOUTH continued this role for the next nine days, spending every night bombarding or on escort or patrol duties. The ship was then withdrawn to the Carrier Battle Group some one hundred and fifty miles to the east of the Falklands, and on 30 May came under Exocet attack by Argentine aircraft. These attacks were fortunately driven off without loss to the Task Force.

The ship returned to San Carlos, during the night of 1 June. The routine of daytime air defence and night time patrolling and probing the enemy continued until 8 June. On that day, whilst bombarding enemy positions, PLYMOUTH was attacked by five Argentinian Mirages whilst alone and outside the sanctuary of the land and seaborne air defences of San Carlos. The ship was struck by four bombs and a large number of cannon shells. PLYMOUTH destroyed two of the attacking aircraft and damaged two others, but was herself damaged. Five casualties were sustained but were rapidly evacuated by helicopter. A bomb which detonated a depth charge on the flight deck caused a serious fire below decks. It took about ninety anxious minutes to extinguish it—with help from nearby ships. A second bomb passed through the ship's funnel without exploding and a further two completely wrecked the anti submarine mortar and its handling equipment, before passing out through the mortar well—again without exploding! Hurried repairs overnight and during the next day left the ship semi-operational and she left San Carlos for more effective repairs. As soon as naval repair personnel in MV STENA SEASPREAD had restored the majority of the ship's fighting capability, she was back on the gunline off Stanley on the night of 14 June when the Argentinian garrison surrendered.

HMS PLYMOUTH entered Stanley Harbour on 17 June, the first British warship to do so, to assist in setting up the naval control of the harbour. After a brief spell back in San Carlos for further minor repairs, the ship left the Task Force on 21 June to return with HMS GLAMORGAN, another battle casualty, to the UK, via Ascension Island and Gibraltar.

HMS PLYMOUTH returned to Rosyth on 14 July for much needed docking and repairs, having steamed 34,000 miles since leaving her home port in March. During her operations in the South Atlantic, PLYMOUTH fired 909 4.5" shells, mainly supporting military operations ashore and nine Seacat missiles. She shot down five enemy aircraft. A fine record for another old lady of the Task Force.

HMS Plymouth damaged in San Carlos Water being assisted by HMS Avenger.

A sailor peers through the hole in
HMS Plymouth's hull made by a 1,000 bomb.

Another hole—made in HMS Plymouth's flight deck
by a bomb.

## HMS FEARLESS

The 13,000 ton Assault Ship HMS FEARLESS sailed from Portsmouth on April 6 after feverish preparations to embark Commodore Michael Clapp (flying his broad pennant as Commodore Amphibious Warfare), his staff, and elements of 3 Commando Brigade, including its Headquarters. Three Sea King and 3 Scout helicopters of 846 Naval Air Squadron and 3 Commando Brigade were also embarked.

During the routine Ascension "stop over" there was an opportunity for the marines and paras to take much needed exercise. For a lucky few sailors there was the chance to enjoy a tropical beach for two hours, even if it did mean filling sandbags for the ship at the same time!

The approach to San Carlos Water for the overnight assault was in total darkness and almost complete silence. In the early stages FEARLESS and other ships in the anchorage were attacked repeatedly by aircraft of the Argentine Air Force and Navy. FEARLESS herself escaped with slight damage, a few injuries and some very near misses, but she was credited with a share of 4 Argentine jets shot down. The Argentine pilots came to regard the anchorage as "Death Valley" according to one prisoner of war, such were their losses under withering fire from ships and shore.

Once the initial landings were over FEARLESS became Headquarters Ship for Major General Jeremy Moore and his staff, as well as supporting elements of the 5th Infantry Brigade and 846 Naval Air Squadron. The force headquarters' staff remained embarked throughout the land battles. At times the ship was "host" to over 1500 people and the flight deck handled over 5,000 helicopter landings—as well as a passing visit from a Sea Harrier for fuel.

Engineers and firefighters saw service in other ships damaged during the fighting, helping with heavy repairs to bomb damage and being lowered from helicopters to fight fires in ARGONAUT, PLYMOUTH and SIR GALAHAD. FEARLESS also provided a safe haven for survivors of ANTELOPE and some of the lightly injured survivors of the SIR TRISTRAM and SIR GALAHAD tragedies. An Argentine jet pilot, who parachuted injured into San Carlos Water after his Skyhawk was shot down during an attack on the assembled shipping, was also treated on board.

After taking Goose Green, much Argentinian equipment was discovered—repaired by FEARLESS personnel it was soon put to good use. For a short time an Argentine anti-aircraft gun was fitted to the flight deck and manned at action stations, before being passed on to a logistic ship whose need was the greater. A number of helicopters found in working condition, were soon in use, albeit with a new paint scheme. Several

51

ships were also taken, repaired and sailed under the White Ensign with crews from FEARLESS. MV MONSUNNEN, stolen from the Falklanders by the Argentines and the oil rig tender YEHUIN were to be the proud "first commands" for two young officers on board.

There were losses as well as successes, and one of the ship's four landing craft, codenamed Foxtrot Four, was attacked and sunk by Argentine aircraft. The coxswain and five of the crew were killed. A fund was immediately started to help the dependants of those killed and received more than £12,000 within a very few days from the ships' companies of FEARLESS and her sister INTREPID. A typical gesture from ever generous seamen and marines.

After the surrender of the Argentine forces at Stanley, HMS FEARLESS was directed to take General Menendez, the Argentine Commander, and three of his senior staff officers on board as prisoners.

HMS Fearless survives a near miss

## HMS INTREPID

Portsmouth dockyard workers must share the accolade for the quite astonishing feat of bringing the 12,120 ton INTREPID back to life within only 10 days. She was awaiting refit when ordered to join the force, less than half her normal complement was available and she was totally de-fuelled, de-ammunitioned and partially de-stored.

INTREPID sailed for operational sea trials and work up on 15 April before proceeding south on 26 April with the ferry SS NORLAND. Argentine intelligence was probably unaware of the speed which INTREPID was activated, or that she joined the largest British amphibious assault group assembled for 26 years. Preparations for this included the embarkation of the 3rd Battalion, Parachute Regiment from SS CANBERRA on the high seas on 19 May.

The ship's report of "D-Day" reproduced below needs no further comment.

"Our arrival in the Falkland Sound and San Carlos Water took place on a bitterly cold, damp morning. There was little wind and sound travelled far.

With enemy troops in the area we were relieved and surprised to arrive at our allocated anchorage in the Falkland Sound unmolested. To the west, shortly after anchoring, naval gunfire support started near Pebble Island and continued until first light; the sky line being lit like a firework display. At this stage it all still seemed a little distant and unreal. Just after first light, when we shifted anchor into San Carlos Water, the fireworks started for us!

Just after the lunchtime "action snack" came our first sight of the enemy—half a wing of a Pucara was seen above the hill on our port quarter and the Bofors guns opened fire against this target before it dropped behind the hill attempting to attack troops ashore. There were many tense cries of "Alarm Aircraft!" as a bird took to the wing on a distant hill, only to be discounted as the supposedly fast moving target hovered! The main events of the afternoon were attacks by A4 and Mirage aircraft. The immediate thing that comes to mind was the sheer speed and determination of the attacking aircraft—alarm procedures were just fast enough to bring weapons to bear. Aircraft approached along the Falkland Sound, attacking ships en route, and then turned hard right into San Carlos Water where they blitzed amphibious shipping off-loading essential supplies.

Our first raid that afternoon was by Mirages attempting to attack SS CANBERRA and HMS ANTRIM. The port forward Seacat was fired giving us a chance to overcome the butterflies everyone was feeling deep down. It was interesting that once the nerves calmed after the first raids, nobody took cover—they were too busy urging each other to take out the aircraft. The first raid was a great confidence booster, we saw one Mirage turn away and the pilot eject after being hit by Seacats fired by ourselves and HMS PLYMOUTH.

Air activity was continuous throughout the afternoon but the worse moment was when one aircraft crossed the ship's head dropping a pattern of bombs 100 feet from the port bow; another aircraft appeared from nowhere and closed fast. We had that gut feeling success was his for the taking, time stood still . . . The starboard Seacat fired, for what seemed like an eternity the aircraft kept coming with the Seacat closing. Luckily, before releasing his bombs or firing at us, he turned hard right and literally fell out of the sky behind a hill for cover. This was one to us and from then on the confidence and effectiveness of HMS INTREPID's weapons took a definite upward turn. The afternoon continued in a haze of air attacks with little time to collect one's thoughts before the next alarm. By dusk all involved were exhausted and it was a great relief when darkness fell and we relaxed with the knowledge the Argentinians only had a limited night flying capability.

We were at Action Stations at first light the next day for what proved to be an anti-climax. The Argentinians were obviously taking stock. The only raid was at dusk, by two Skyhawks, which was ineffective.   The third day almost came as light relief with attacks by A4s. A lucky day for us as bombs fell short by 100 feet and spent Seacats straddled us. It was not uncommon for 4.5 inch shells from our own ships to travel over the hill from the Falkland Sound into Bomb Alley. Fortunately no one was hit. This was the last day the Argentinians attacked against minimum resistance; the Rapier batteries were not yet fully established ashore. After a forenoon attack the A4s were far too close for comfort, but the afternoon was to become even more awe-inspiring.

One particular raid of A4s and Mirages crossed the bay ahead of HMS INTREPID as a Mirage passed over HMS ANTELOPE, clipping her mainmast and bending it, before bursting into a burning mass of metal. This aircraft had been hit by a Seawolf from HMS BROADSWORD but not before it had laid a pattern of bombs over HMS ANTELOPE. During this particular afternoon raid, our starboard Bofors sliced off an aircraft wing tip before it disappeared over the hillside.

Another evening, later that week, saw a daring raid by the Argentinians on Ajax Bay at dusk when Skyhawks accurately bombed our ammunition supplies and caused several casualties. This was an impressive performance, the A4s came in very low and managed to avoid detection until they were actually in San Carlos Water. HMS INTREPID can claim to have hit both these aircraft with Bofors gunfire. The ammunition explosions ashore went on long into the evening . . .

During this time at San Carlos INTREPID's landing craft were constantly busy ferrying mountains of stores, personnel and even acted as minesweepers.

Between 19 May and 18 June over 4,300 people were ferried to and from INTREPID by landing craft and helicopter, 1575 of these (and one dog) were Argentinian prisoners brought back from West Falkland. The 4 Sea King helicopters from INTREPID assumed a Jekyll and Hyde existence fulfilling mundane tasks by day then carrying out Special Forces operations at night. On many occasions members of the ship's company helped other units which had been damaged. Welding by shipwrights was often carried out close to explosives, around unexploded bombs and next to fuel tanks . . .

Once the surrender had been signed INTREPID became responsible for the "return to normality" of most of the Falklands. Thirty five communities were visited and assistance given.

A "Sea King Supermarket" was provided to ease basic shortages in the settlements. One working party even managed to deliver a large birthday cake to a small boy by helicopter.

The civilian support task was completed on 22nd June and INTREPID sailed to Port William so her landing craft and working parties could off load a large amount of airfield engineering stores from ATLANTIC CAUSEWAY. This 2½ day task was actually completed in 30 hours—it was time to sail for home—the thought had everyone working just that bit harder . . ."

# HMS ARDENT—THE FINAL CURTAIN . . .

HMS ARDENT beat off 16 Argentine air attacks and was still firing her machine guns and 20 mm cannon when aircraft approached for the 17th and last time. Heavy bombing caused immense damage to the ship and she had to be abandoned. Twenty-two of her ship's company had died.

She had led the amphibious task force down through the Falkland Sound in darkness on May 21, shepherding the ships to their anchorage and beachhead. From there she sped off to bombard Goose Green and enemy troops at Darwin and to harass Argentinian aircraft and military reinforcements. It was only one-and-a-half hours after first light when the first aircraft—a Pucara—homed in on her. More raids were to follow. The ARDENT spent most of the day in Falkland Sound in a deliberate and successful attempt to draw fire and attacks away from the landing force. The Pucara raids were followed quickly by Mirages and Skyhawks, which straddled the ship with two 500 lb bombs. Meanwhile, ARDENT's gunfire support at Goose Green knocked out at least one Pucara on the ground.

As the attacks came faster, two Skyhawks attacked together. Unfortunately, one hit her with two 500 lb. bombs. These caused a large amount of damage aft, writing off the aft missile system. She was soon on fire. Damage control teams soon got the fires under control, but as the frigate headed for the anchorage three Skyhawks attacked from astern, hitting with two 500 lb. bombs. Retard bombs struck the ship's sides.

Despite these attacks, HMS ARDENT fought back. Six aircraft attacked within five minutes as the bombs rained into the water around the ship.

With two hours to dusk, the ship ablaze aft of the funnel, and all power gone, the captain ordered the anchor to be dropped and the men to abandon ship. Right to the end the weapons crew continued firing 20 mm cannon and machine guns.

## HMS ARROW

Befitting her name, HMS ARROW was at the very forefront of the earliest actions. Arriving at Port Stanley on 1 May with Battle Ensigns flying, she bombarded Port Stanley Airport; it was during this daring daytime engagement that ARROW became the first casualty of the Falklands campaign when attacked by Mirage fighters. She survived the attack but incurred the first casualty of the conflict when AB Ian Britnell was wounded. Fortunately he proved to be the only ARROW casualty of the campaign.

HMS ARROW in the three months of the operation steamed 30,000 miles, her engines and weapon systems remaining continuously on line and her men continuously on call—a fine achievement.

HMS Arrow. Every picture tells its own story . . .

## HMS AMBUSCADE
### SOME FACTS AND FIGURES

| | |
|---|---|
| Miles travelled | 29,226 miles |
| Continuous days at sea since leaving Gibraltar | 83 days |

**MEDICAL**

| | |
|---|---|
| Patients seen | 101 |
| Codines issued (mainly ops room crew!) | 200 approx |
| Sea sick pills (mainly Scots Guards and RMs of course) | 400 |

**MAIL RECEIVED** 106 sacks

**ELECTRICITY USED** 1,726,210 Kw

**FUEL USED** 5044.76 tons

**COMMUNICATIONS**

| | |
|---|---|
| Teleprinter rolls used | 17,500 yds |
| Classified signals distributed | 19,128 |

**FLIGHT**

| | |
|---|---|
| Hours flown | 167 |
| Deck landings | 377 |

## FOOD CONSUMED

| | |
|---|---|
| Eggs | 20,000 |
| Meat | 11,000 lbs. |
| Chickens | 1,000 |
| Sausages | 2,000 |
| Baked beans | 2,800 cans |
| Tomatoes | 2,000 cans |
| Milk | 10,800 pints |
| Potatoes | 33,800 lbs. |
| Bread baked | 2,500 loaves |
| Bread rolls | 12,000 |

**NAAFI PURCHASES**

| | |
|---|---|
| Chocolate | 25,812 bars |
| Sweets | 28,880 bags |
| Soft drinks | 12,480 tins |
| Beer | 19,200 tins |
| Pot noodles | 552 |
| Crisps | 5,233 bags |
| Cigarettes | 345,000 |
| Cigars | 3,350 |

**AMMUNITION EXPENDED**

| | |
|---|---|
| 4.5″ shells | 500 |
| Torpedo | 1 |
| Seacat missile | 1 |
| Small arms | Just too many to count! |

## HMS ACTIVE

On the evening of 25 May HMS ACTIVE entered the Total Exclusion Zone just seven days after leaving Ascension and seven hours after the sinking of COVENTRY—it was a clear dark night with a million stars twinkling out of a winter sky.

ACTIVE's employment during the main battle phase fell into a regular pattern. On the Task Force screen during daylight hours (1130-1930) operating 150-180 miles east of Stanley—then detached on operational sorties at night close to the coast. This pattern of operations had been developed to counter the threat from Argentinian air attack during daylight hours.

Having arrived in the area four days after the beachhead at Port San Carlos had been established, ACTIVE's night operations were convoy protection during the re-supply of the beachhead, and shore bombardment prior to the re-capture of Port Stanley.

Inbound convoys normally departed from the edge of the TEZ at approximately 1800 and followed set routes along the north coast of East Falkland to arrive at Teal Inlet or Port San Carlos by 1000 next day. Outbound convoys departed at 2200 to arrive back at the Battle Group by 1100. Escorts normally exchanged convoys at approximately 0300 at the crossover point.

Shore bombardment was normally carried out during the night on the Port Fitzroy gunline (south of Stanley) or the Volunteer Bay/Berkley Sound gunlines (north of Stanley). 0200-0600 was the favourite time to keep the Argentines awake as shells exploded around them ashore.

Naval Gunfire Liaison Officers were embarked for all naval gunfire support operations and proved invaluable in establishing effective liaison with the spotters ashore. This was the first effective test under live conditions for the Navy's digital gun system. It proved itself to be more than a match for the enemy—laying down a withering amount of explosives on such targets as troop and gun emplacements, vehicles, radar sites and ammunition dumps. In particular, on the night of 13/14 June in the calm waters of Berkley Sound and under a full moon, four ships including ACTIVE fired over 1000 rounds into the Moody Brook/Tumbledown area of Stanley and, as it was later learned, contributed greatly to the swift surrender of Argentine Forces on 14 June.

With the soldiers poised on the hills overlooking Stanley and ships on the gunlines either side of the peninsula the final push began. What a night the 13/14 June was with the Army batteries pounding the enemy troops from the hills and four frigates pounding them from seaward. The accuracy of the ships gunfire enabled the troops to move forward rapidly and with great determination. It was like a spectacular firework display with flashes of gunfire and tracer lighting up the night sky. It was a memorable end to the battle—the next day the Argentines finally surrendered. It was all over. HMS ACTIVE returned to the screen and for the first time experienced the kind of weather everyone had been forecasting—a first class gale. She wallowed around for two days fully alert—just in case the Argentinians tried a final attack.

After days reorganising, repairing and a period at Stanley, it was time to think about the long voyage home. There was one final sad journey to make. On the evening of 13 July, ACTIVE detached to San Carlos to visit the memorial to the brave men of ARDENT and ANTELOPE, erected on the windswept hill above Ajax Bay. On the 14 July, grouped around the simple stone cairn dominated by its plain steel cross set amidst the snow-covered heather, men joined in prayer for those who had lost their lives in the battle to establish the bridgehead at San Carlos. A simple wreath of heather was laid, the mournful strains of the Last Post rang out over the wintry waters of Falkland Sound. At 0830 the next morning, in company with MINERVA, the ship sailed quietly from San Carlos Water—for home.

HMS Active—her 4.5 inch gun bombarding an Argentine shore position.

# HMS ANTELOPE

Both of the two 1,000 lb. bombs which struck HMS ANTELOPE as she guarded the entrance to San Carlos Water failed to explode on impact. Tragically one was triggered as bomb disposal experts attempted to defuse it. The ship was torn open, she burst into flame, and later sank.

She had been an air defence picket, protecting the vulnerable landing ships in San Carlos Water. "The idea was to put a cork in the bottle and bottle up the entrance to San Carlos Water," said Commander Nick Tobin, the frigate's Commanding Officer. "Attacking aircraft would have to fly over us and through our anti-aircraft barrage before they could get to the amphibious ships."

They were attacked by one aircraft which came in at 30 feet above the water. It was engaged by one of the ship's 20 mm cannons. It dropped two bombs, one of which flew between the two masts and the other hit the ship on the starboard side. This aircraft was hit with about eight 20 mm shells, it then struck the main mast and disintegrated in a ball of flame. But the ship was attacked again by two other aircraft, these were deterred by a Seacat missile and fire from the 4.5 inch gun. Then they were attacked again and another bomb entered the ship. All these attacks were coordinated and very professionally carried out by the Argentine pilots. Two Army bomb disposal experts, Warrant Officer Phillips and Staff Sergeant Jim Prescott embarked to tackle these bombs after HMS ANTELOPE limped back into San Carlos Water.

They started with the first bomb which was lodged over the engine room and made several attempts to defuse it using various methods, but it exploded and blew a hole in the ships side from waterline to funnel. Fires started in the engine room and spread very quickly. Staff Sergeant Prescott was killed and WO Phillips had lost an arm. The ships' company fought the fires and tried to contain the damage but it was a losing battle, many vital systems including the fire main and electrical supplies were cut off. It soon became apparent the ship would have to be abandoned. The ship's company were picked up by landing craft.

Throughout the night the ship blazed and as the fire reached magazine after magazine the explosions could be heard throughout the anchorage. Next day she eventually sank in a cloud of steam and smoke. For a while her bows and stern stuck up through the water in a giant defiant V before they too slipped beneath the surface.

After the explosion.

The last moments.

# HMS COVENTRY

HMS COVENTRY, was the first warship to fire the Sea Dart and Sea Skua missiles in action. Both were highly successful.

On 1 May HMS COVENTRY, as an advanced air defence picket, was the first ship to enter the Total Exclusion Zone around the Falklands, and she remained within this war zone under constant air, surface and submarine threat until she was sunk by enemy bombers 24 days later.

From the first day she was closely involved in the air battle and successfully controlled and directed Sea Harrier aircraft against enemy aircraft. She also carried out the first surface action of the war when in the early morning of 3 May her Lynx helicopter detected a suspicious surface contact on its radar. Armed with Sea Skua missiles it scored two direct hits on an enemy patrol vessel which was totally destroyed—the explosion being seen 30 miles away by ships of the Task Force. This vessel was attempting to bring fuel and ammunition to the Argentinian troops at Stanley.

A week after entering the battle zone COVENTRY was tasked to bombard the Port Stanley area with her 4.5 inch gun and to engage enemy re-supply aircraft with Sea Dart missiles. She was escorted by HMS BROADSWORD to provide close air defence with Sea Wolf missiles. During one of the days on the "gunline" a 5 aircraft Argentinian re-supply mission was thwarted when COVENTRY attacked with Sea Dart. One missile, at its maximum range, exploded close to 2 aircraft and brought them down, the remainder turned away and ran for home. Two hours later a troop carrying helicopter was also destroyed by a Sea Dart missile.

During the same busy day COVENTRY directed a Sea Harrier out to the spy ship NARWHAL which had been gathering intelligence about the Task Force. This attack caused severe damage to the NARWHAL leading to its capture and subsequent sinking.

In the last week of her life, COVENTRY operated with BROADSWORD to the north of the Falklands co-ordinating air defence of the amphibious fleet and landing force in the Falkland Sound. On 24 May 2 Sea Harriers were directed on to a raid of 4 aircraft and shot down 3 of them with Sidewinder missiles and 30mm guns. The fourth aircraft fled for home. In the same afternoon Rapier missiles ashore and the ships in the Sound are believed to have destroyed a further 6 aircraft.

On the next day, which was to be her last, COVENTRY was again about 12 miles north of the Sound, with BROADSWORD, when two enemy Skyhawk aircraft were detected and engaged with Sea Dart missiles and both destroyed. In the afternoon the ship was in action again when two more aircraft were reported by ships in Falkland Sound. As they left the Sound they were engaged with Sea Dart and one was brought down.

That evening two very low flying enemy aircraft came off the coast heading towards COVENTRY and BROADSWORD. A defending barrage of close range weapons was put up by COVENTRY which forced the aircraft to veer towards BROADSWORD. BROADSWORD was hit but did not suffer any casualties or major damage; both aircraft were hit by gunfire. Almost immediately afterwards a further pair of aircraft launched a very fast and low attack against COVENTRY during which she was straffed by cannon fire and hit by 3 bombs which blew out a large part of the port side. This severe damage caused the ship to take on a heavy list to port within a few minutes and all power was lost. Some fifteen minutes later the ship capsized and after a further fifteen minutes all that could be seen of the ship was the keel about six feet above the sea. The ship was abandoned and 275 survivors including the injured jumped into the freezing sea and swam to liferafts. The speedy arrival of boats from BROADSWORD and helicopters from shore resulted in the recovery of all survivors within 90 minutes and before nightfall. They were lifted to BROADSWORD and the injured taken to the Field Hospital ashore or to the Hospital ship UGANDA.

Tragically 19 men lost their lives during the attack and a further 25 were injured. Of the 4 aircraft that attacked the ship in her last action it was learnt later that 2 failed to return to their bases. By the time it was dark the air raids had ceased and BROADSWORD headed for San Carlos Water to transfer the survivors to RFA FORT AUSTIN. They were later transferred to QE 2 at South Georgia for the passage home to UK.

HMS COVENTRY, the anti-aircraft cruiser of World War 2, distinguished herself in the Mediterranean and was finally lost in action against dive bomber aircraft forty years ago. In the same way her successor went down fighting and in only four weeks of war had shot down 5 fighter bombers, a helicopter, sunk a patrol vessel and controlled numerous Sea Harriers which accounted for several more enemy aircraft. A fine record for a fine ship.

**HMS COVENTRY**—The last half hour
Bombed and on fire the ship looses all power . . .

and slowly rolls over as liferafts are launched . . .

helicopters arrive for a major Search & Rescue
operation around the upturned hull.

Four of the Trawler/minesweepers steaming in line abreast.

# MCMV

One of the Task Force's most unlikely units—the 11th Minecountermeasures Squadron—consisted of five Humberside trawlers hastily converted into minesweepers. Fully commissioned into the Royal Navy they were thus the only commercial vessels which could use the prefix HMS.

Apart from sweeping 20 mines in two minefields the Squadron—HMS CORDELLA, HMS JUNELLA, HMS FARNELLA, HMS NORTHELLA and HMS PICT were involved in night-time landings of special forces behind enemy lines. The Squadron became "maids of all work", carrying out stores transfers, delivering mail and topping up fresh water tanks. They helped transfer troops of 5 Infantry Brigade at South Georgia from QE 2 to CANBERRA and NORLAND despite gale force winds.

At one stage, HMS PICT landed most of her ship's company because of the danger of being sunk when clearing a particularly hazardous minefield. She was manned by 14 volunteers—the minimum necessary to run the ship and sweep the mines.

HMS JUNELLA was eventually ordered to bring home for examination one Argentinian mine. A suitable specimen was towed ashore by dinghy, defused on the beach and later hoisted onto HMS JUNELLA's stern. She sailed the 8,000 miles home with this mine still packed with explosive. To keep it cool and safe in the tropics it was covered with mattresses constantly soaked with sea water.

Heavy weather in the South Atlantic was just as uncomfortable as it is in the fishing grounds of the North Atlantic.

The minesweeper support ship St Helena—the merchantman which normally plies between that island and UK—replenishing the minecountermeasure vessels HMS Ledbury and HMS Brecon. They were late arrivals in the South Atlantic.

An "Honours Board" of mines swept—painted on one trawler's bridge.

# THE RED CROSS FLEET . . .

### HMS HYDRA—HMS HERALD—HMS HECLA

Britain's first hospital ship for 30 years (the last was the Maine, sent to Korea in 1952), the UGANDA left Gibraltar on April 19, followed a day later by HMS HECLA and from Portsmouth on April 24 by her sister ships HERALD and HYDRA.

They had been converted to their new roles for the Falklands emergency and headed south in their new "Red Cross" colours.

HERALD had returned to Portsmouth from a seven month deployment in the Gulf just 17 days before she sailed for the South Atlantic in company with her sister ship.

On board, HECLA, HYDRA and HERALD were an extra surgeon-lieutenant, and three medical assistants, in addition to the normal medical team of one surgeon-lieutenant and one leading medical assistant. Some 30 of the crew were trained to act as nurses to supplement the medical staff.

The wardroom and ship's company dining hall were converted into wards capable of holding 50 seriously wounded with space for a further 50 to 100 "walking wounded" in messdecks.

CANBERRA, requisitioned earlier from P & O, was earmarked the centre for casualties from any assault on the Falklands. A large medical team including surgeons, technicians, nursing staff and Royal Marines musicians doubling as stretcher-bearers had joined the liner as she sailed from Southampton.

A hospital unit had been set up in the liner's stadium just below the forward helicopter landing pad.

The pattern which developed was for land casualties both British and captured Argentinians to be taken from the field hospital at Ajax Bay to SS UGANDA. Once their condition had stabilized 100 at a time were taken by the converted survey ships on a four-day passage from SS UGANDA to Montivideo to be repatriated. Naval casualties were taken direct to SS UGANDA.

Eventually two Argentine hospital ships—BAHIA PARAISO and ALMIRANTE IRIZAR arrived in the area, patients were then segregated nationally. Throughout the conflict, hospital ships operated freely together, transferring medical stores as needed and cross operating ambulance helicopters.

The detailed story of HMS HYDRA provides an illuminating insight into the work of the Survey Ships in their new role of floating ambulances.

HMS HYDRA was ordered to stop her survey work off the west coast of Scotland, and to prepare to sail from Portsmouth on 24 April as a hospital ship to the South Atlantic. Plans were rapidly formulated to replace an unservicable main engine and to take onboard large quantities of medical stores and cold weather clothing. Food for six months was embarked and stowed in any, and every, conceivable space. Ship's fittings were removed or modified to ease the handling of stretchers, and, even after sailing, work continued to convert certain spaces for use as casualty wards and emergency operating theatres.

The entire external surface of the ship had to be painted white with identifying red crosses; and the dockyard fitted a strong point on the port boat deck, and cut away part of a nearby bulwark for underway replenishment equipment.

The last stores were embarked and the last dockyard matey left the ship only minutes before sailing at 1000 on Saturday 24 April with HMS HERALD in company to a rousing and colourful departure.

Both ships set course for Freetown, Sierra Leone, remaining clear of the major shipping routes, a brief stop was made to fuel and water ship. Next stop was Ascension Island on 8 May, where the ships anchored to embark last minute stores from an RAF Chinook helicopter. The future task was yet to be defined in detail. However, it was clear that the ship must be prepared to receive, treat, care for and despatch large numbers of, possibly, raw casualties, by day and by night, in a potentially hostile environment and in bad weather. Additionally, the ship had to be able to replenish liquids and light solids underway—evolutions unknown in the "Survey Navy".

As the battle ashore developed, so the waiting hospital ships (UGANDA, HECLA, HYDRA and HERALD) moved closer to the islands. On 30 May, a Red Cross Box (RCB) was established some 15 miles to the north of East Falkland Island. From the RCB, the hospital ships were withdrawn periodically to other areas to deal with casualities or to replenish stores and fuel.

It soon became clear that casualties from the field hospital established ashore at Ajax Bay could be transferred direct to UGANDA, in large numbers using troop carrying helicopters. The survey ambulance ships, well illuminated at night, embarked up to 100 stabilised casualties at a time from UGANDA, and took them on the four day passage to Montevideo, from where they were flown home to Brize Norton by RAF VC-10 Medevac aircraft. The ship, meanwhile, returned south and prepared for the next casualty evacuation.

In the initial stages of the military operation, British hospital ships, in accordance with the Geneva Convention, treated both British and Argentinian victims. When the two Argentinian hospital ships—BAHIA PARALSO and ALMIRANTE IRIZAR appeared in the area, patients were segregated nationally. Throughout the conflict, hospital ships of both nations operated freely together, transferring medical stores when a need was identified and allowing cross operation of ambulance helicopters.

By the time hostilities ceased on land, on 14 June, each of the three Ambulance Ships—HECLA, HYDRA and HERALD—had completed two runs to Montevideo, but the medical team in UGANDA continued to work at more than full stretch and the survey ships continued to ferry casualties out of the area—the fighting had stopped but the fight was still on to save life . . .

RFA Olmeda replenishing HMS Hydra and SS Uganda with fuel.

# Lifeline of the Fleet—
# The Royal Fleet Auxiliaries . . .

## MEGA RAS—RFA FORT AUSTIN/FORT GRANGE

The RFA is the civilian afloat support arm of the Fleet and is a world leader in the skill 'RAS'—Replenishment at Sea. In all weathers these merchant ships (with their embarked stores party of civil servants) manoeuvre to within 200 ft of a Naval ship and both maintain the same course and speed whilst transferring fuel, food, ammunition and other solid stores. Wherever Naval ships go there goes the RFA too—they were in the thick of the action in San Carlos Water and elsewhere. Sadly too, they shared the tragedy in the attack on RFA's SIR GALAHAD and SIR TRISTRAM at Bluff Cove.

Like all ships in the operation FORT AUSTIN performed near miracles of effort and endurance, but for her it started well before the Naval action. In mid April whilst topping up the ships of the Task Force she stored a series of ships in a continuous operation for over 26 hours. As one RN ship broke off another took her place alongside. The operation has since come to be known as the 'megaras'—a record breaking gigantic replenishment at sea.

Her sister ship RFA FORT GRANGE sailed from the United Kingdom on Friday 14th May 1982 after completing refit one month early, and loading maximum cargo in record time. "C" Flight of 824 Squadron embarked with 3 Sea Kings, and the journey south was spent training the new ship's company in basic drills and emergency exercises.

On the long journey south FORT GRANGE was oveflown by an Argentinian Hercules. Fortunately it did not drop any bombs, but later bombed the BRITISH WYE in the same area.

The ship arrived in the Total Exclusion Zone on 3rd June to rendezvous with the Carrier Group—in thick fog. Being the first auxiliary stores ship to arrive in the TEZ since the Task Force sailed she was bulging at the seams with stores and "goodies". Many of the Carrier Group ships were so short of food they were about to break open the emergency "compo" rations. FORT GRANGE spent eight hectic days replenishing them using both helicopters and alongside replenishment methods. In addition, two aircraft were on anti-submarine patrol. During this period 25 ships were resupplied with vital stores.

After transferring hundreds of tons of stores she sailed into Bomb Alley to resupply the beach head and the ships of Bomb Alley.

The next few weeks alternated between Rasing and Vertreps (stores transfer by helicopter) with the Battle Group, visits to San Carlos Water to top up RFA's going home, and embark new stores brought from the UK. GEESTPORT, LYCAON, SAXONIA and AVELONA STAR were regular "customers". During the spells in San Carlos Water she supplied stores to Army and Navy Helicopter detachments, and the PoW Camps. On one occasion she steamed round to Bluff Cove to Vertrep tons of victuals to RFA SIR GERIANT who was supporting a number of soldiers and trying to get the bomb damaged RFA SIR TRISTRAM serviceable again.

On 11th July 1982 while Vertrepping stores from HMS LEEDS CASTLE one of the Sea Kings ditched. The crew were picked up by HMS LEEDS CASTLE's searider, but the helicopter sank in the heavy swell.

In all, the ship was involved in five air raids but was not actually attacked in any of them. RFA FORT GRANGE spent 107 days in the Total Exclusion Zone during which time she carried out the following:-

208 transfers with 42 HM Ships                2 transfers with 1 Royal Marine Auxiliary Service ship
 65 transfers with 18 Royal Fleet Auxiliary vessels   29 transfers with 7 shore stations
 75 transfers with 29 Merchant vessels        10 major consolidations with 7 ships

She issued the fleet with about 700,000 lbs of potatoes and half a million eggs—some ships must have been virtually living on egg 'n chips. Also issued were 10,500 gallons of draught beer and 21,000 cases of canned beer (at 24 cans per case).

The Flight flew 334 day sorties and 63 night sorties, a total of 867 hours day flying and 154 hours night flying. All this entailed 933 day deck landings and 165 night landings. In addition to this, each time the ship went into either Port San Carlos or Stanley she became the local Spar ship and Heron garage with customers arriving from all directions for food, petrol, a shower and drinks/lunch

RFA Fort Grange—'the floating supermarket'—in San Carlos Water.

# RFA STROMNESS

On 2nd April RFA STOMNESS lay in Portsmouth dockyard, destored prior to disposal, a victim of defence cuts. By 7th April STROMNESS, restored with her vast "supermarket" range of stores including 15,000 man-months of food, part of one of her holds converted into a dormitory, over 350 members of 45 Commando Royal Marines embarked; had set sail south to join the Task Force.

The cargo, 2750 tons of it; included equipment, stores and ammunition for the embarked troops. On deck were stacks of aluminium sheeting which when linked together formed an "Airport 82", the portable airstrip which, along with the emergency fuel handling equipment, was landed on the Falklands for the Harriers.

On "D-Day", 21 May, STROMNESS sailed into Falkland Sound (STROMNESS was the first RFA to enter the Sound) along with her escorts, to anchor and to disgorge her Royal Marines into LCU's for the beach assault. Five of the next six days were spent in San Carlos Water discharging stores, ammunition and the airfield (soon to be set up as "San Carlos Airport"). Cargo work continued during the air-raids as stores were craned into mexefloates and LCU's, more ammunition, stores and rations (including fresh bread rolls daily) were airlifted from the ship's flightdeck to 45 Commando Marines dug-in on the surrounding hillsides protecting the anchorage. The ships at anchor in San Carlos Water were under most constant air attack as wave after wave of Mirage and Skyhawk aircraft bombed their way through the air defences. By this time STROMNESS mounted 18 General purpose Machine Guns for her own air defence, one of which accounted for the Mirage that dropped four bombs (only one of which went off) alongside the ship—between her and the ammunition ship RFA RESOURCE. Both were discharging ammunition at the time.

On completion of her task in San Carlos STROMNESS sailed for South Georgia taking the survivors from HMS COVENTRY to join the QE 2 awaiting at anchor there. Having transferred the survivors and embarking over 400 further troops from QE 2 and large quantities of ammunition and Rapier missiles from LYCAON, STROMNESS sailed once more for San Carlos. On the way back STROMNESS topped-up HM Ships, RFA's and MN ships with food and stores (her more normal every-day task of Fleet Support).

Back in San Carlos it was a case of landing the troops and ammunition before rejoining the Battle Group to re-supply them with food and stores. This was followed by another trip to South Georgia in whose more sheltered waters STROMNESS re-stored herself from the MV SAXONIA (which took four days). Then it was back to the Falklands, this time Port Stanley to replenish ships now anchored there, (the surrender having taken place) and to land food and stores for the troops ashore.

Port Stanley also saw the return of the 45 Commando Royal Marines, who had landed from STROMNESS some four weeks earlier at San Carlos and had "Yomped" their way across the East Falklands. It was then homeward bound for the ship and the Marines they left at Ascension for their flight home—STROMNESS continued north to Portsmouth and an overwhelming reception.

Aerial photograph of HMS Intrepid replenishing from RFA Stromness taken by one of her four Sea Kings.

# R.F.A. BLUE ROVER

RFA BLUE ROVER completed a Gulf of Hormuz patrol in March 82 and was returning to the United Kingdom via Exercise Springtrain when the Falklands crisis developed. The exercise was terminated and most ships immediately deployed south.

BLUE ROVER felt "very much the odd man out" being ordered to return to Portsmouth. However before the ships parted BLUE ROVER transferred virtually every pint of fuel, item of stores and victuals to ships proceeding south in a "mega" replenishment. Back in Portsmouth BLUE ROVER began storing ship with at least six months supplies. Loading cargo and stores for ships deployed and converting to an aviation spirit and petrol carrier.

By 16th April, fully fuelled, stored, victualled, BLUE ROVER, too, deployed south. This fast turn round was only possible due to the magnificent assistance from Portsmouth Dockyard and the RN Field Gun crews who provided the additional manpower to strike down and stow the mountain of cargo and stores, with which she was now crammed.

BLUE ROVER sailed to Ascension Island and received yet more stores and equipment for ships to the south and fuelled the LSL's of the amphibious force. From Ascension she went indirectly to South Georgia, juggling fuel and stores with various consorts to again become a "modified fleet tanker".

In South Georgia, BLUE ROVER came under the tactical command of HMS ENDURANCE and with her formed the afloat support for the garrison on the island. During her stay in South Georgia she refuelled various ships and tugs arriving from the north and spent time at sea plotting icebergs and pack ice to warn approaching shipping—including QE 2 and CANBERRA.

Following the land assault on the Falklands, the ground forces were short of ammunition and BLUE ROVER was tasked to take a load to the islands.

BLUE ROVER entered San Carlos Water, for the first time on 1st June and was a regular visitor thereafter—virtually every other day fuelling all ships and supplying the Army with aviation spirit, petrol and diesel by Bowser and Dracones; she was so much in demand she was usually "sucked dry" every two days. The flight deck was in constant use and became a mini airport, supplying dozens of aircraft with fuel as well as hot food and showers and stores to aircrews and marines.

She seemed to become a favourite stopping place for the aircrews. During one particular arduous day of fuelling and flying operations, one Sea King landed on for fuel and a scruffy, muddy, tired pilot asked if his crew could have a few sandwiches, the look of absolute amazement on the aircrew's faces as an immaculate steward came onto the flight deck with a silver tray covered by a white napkin and a freshly cooked meal made the leg pull worthwhile.

After the surrender of the Argentine forces, BLUE ROVER moved round to Port Stanley and continued the same job until 28th June, when orders were received for her to proceed back to the United Kingdom in company with HMS ANTRIM.

BLUE ROVER was a lucky ship throughout—coming under air attack only once by high level bombers.

Not many onboard even dared to think of the consequences should she have been hit at any stage. Petrol, aviation fuel and ammunition do not make for a particularly safe cargo!


## RFA BAYLEAF—some maiden voyage . . .

One of the most remarkable achievements of the RFA's deployment to the South Atlantic was that of the brand new tanker BAYLEAF. Within three weeks of being accepted from the builders she was fully operational, stored—and on her way south.

The 37,000 ton tanker supported the carriers HMS HERMES, HMS INVINCIBLE and their escorts. She also replenished the QE II and topped up her own tanks from civilian tankers inexperienced in replenishment at sea. These replenishments between unweildy ships in appalling weather and sea states were a considerable success. Her first task was the replenishment of the QE II which lasted 11 hours, again in appalling weather.

Despite continuously steaming 30,000 miles the brand new BAYLEAF didn't miss an operational commitment or suffer any major problems, a significant tribute to her crew and builders—Cammell Laird of Birkenhead.

During the campaign she handled more than 160,000 cubic metres of fuel, and at the height of the crisis she received 1,000 signals a day. She also completed 100 helicopter transfers of stores and drummed oil, not bad for a ship not even designed for helicopter operations.

---

A few simple statistics illustrate the work load of an RFA tanker. RFA OLMEDA spent 96 days at sea during the campaign, steamed 30,000 miles, replenished 185 ships with 64,000 tons fuel, and was replenished herself with 58,000 tons from 10 freighting tankers.

# LANDING SHIPS OF THE FORCE—

## The story from RFA Sir Percivale

RFA SIR PERCIVALE sailed from Marchwood Military Port, Southampton to join the Falklands Task Force. The Logistic Support on board were from 7 different Army and Royal Marine Units.

She spent a night at anchor in Lyme Bay before heading for the R/V off Plymouth to join RFA's SIR GALAHAD, SIR LANCELOT, SIR GERIANT and PEARLEAF and HMS FEARLESS.

She arrived in Ascension Island and anchored in Clarence Bay, and was joined by RFA STROMNESS and FORT AUSTIN—and MV ELK. One the 28th April FORT TORONTO arrived carrying the much needed fresh water for the forces at this island base.

During her stay there she re-distributed cargo and troops and uplifted extra stores. This complicated task was carried out by helicopters, Mexe floats and local craft. A Bofors gun was fitted on the starboard side of the fo'c'st'le—machine guns formed the rest of the "main armament". An air defence team of Royal Navy and 40 Commando Marine gunners boarded and manned this equipment.

Towards the end of this period she carried out an exercise which entailed airlifting by helicopter 7 Battery equipment and troops ashore, simulating her eventual task in the Falklands. It was completed even though 25 loads had to be lifted—in 40 minutes.

RFA SIR PERCIVALE sailed from Ascension Island in company with RFA's SIR LANCELOT, TRISTRAM, GALAHAD, GERIANT and PEARLEAF, under the command of HMS ANTELOPE on April 29th.

The ship's officers were taught how to use and look after the weapons which were placed on the bridge. The 3 Gazelle helicopters had been armed with two rocket pods and began firing practice.

Never before had 105mm field guns been fired at sea, but his whole expedition was full of "firsts" and the RFA fired its first broadside using 105mm guns of 7 Battery. A spectacular and successful exercise.

HMS ANTELOPE was relieved by HMS ANTRIM which took the group to the main body of the Task Force. The final approach to the R/V and to the landing was made from well to the east, staying out of aircraft range for as long as possible.

## D—Day

Early morning raids captured Fanning Head on the day of the landings. It was very quiet as SIR PERCIVALE led the other landing ships towards Falkland Sound.

On the way into San Carlos Water SIR PERCIVALE passed CANBERRA, RFA STROMNESS and HMS FEARLESS at anchor in North Falkland Sound and then NORLAND and HMS INTREPID at the entrance to San Carlos Water. The bad weather of the previous days had gone and left a cloudless moonlit starry sky! Not the ideal conditions for remaining unseen. The silence was only broken by sounds of gunfire and flashes of tracer, the only indication that fighting had started.

She arrived at her anchorage off Ajax Bay as an LCU approached the beach. At first light the Mexe float was dropped and the loading started. The Gazelle helicopters took off to give air support and the Sea Kings and Wessex started airlifting troops and stores ashore.

At about 12.40 the first Air Raid Warning was raised. A Pucara appeared over the ridge. The pilot seemed more surprised than us and promptly ditched his load into the hills and disappeared rapidly to the south.

At 15.00 the first heavy air attack took place. Numerous Mirage and Skyhawks attacked the ships in San Carlos and Falkland Sound—as well recorded elsewhere.

Despite these heavy air attacks work continued and more and more equipment and troops were landed from the amphibious group. Helicopters flew continuously during the day. Rapier missile sites were set up as gun batteries and troops dug in.

That night the ships shifted anchorage in an attempt to make it difficult for the aircraft to pinpoint specific targets next day.

Sunday 23 May began quietly but by lunchtime the amphibious force suffered heavy air attacks yet again.

The determination and bravery of the Argentine pilots cannot be denied. They were having a reasonable rate of success, albeit suffering heavy losses themselves. One aircraft which overflew HMS ANTELOPE was caught in heavy cross-fire and the aircraft disintegrated in a ball of flame. It was time to shift berth again . . .

San Carlos Water on the afternoon of Monday 24 May was again attacked by waves of Mirages and Skyhawks and for the first time they attacked from the south. It very quickly became obvious that the primary targets were now the Landing Ships.

RFA's SIR GALAHAD, SIR LANCELOT and SIR BEDIVERE were anchored in a line running north/south, on the western side while SIR PERCIVALE was on the opposite side in Fern Valley Creek.

As the aircraft flew northward everything opened fire. A Wessex V helicopter was very nearly hit as it ducked down to sea level to keep clear. A Blowpipe missile launched from SIR PERCIVALE was skilfully manoeuvred over the helicopter then turned through 90° to give chase to a Mirage. The missile detonated in the proximity of the tail of the aircraft and large pieces of the tail were seen to break off. The aircraft began smoking badly and was seen to disappear over the hills. It was later confirmed that the aircraft had crashed.

During this run SIR LANCELOT and SIR GALAHAD were hit and both had unexploded bombs on board.

More dropped bombs narrowly missed RFA STROMNESS and RESOURCE. No other ships suffered damage. The intensity of fire was sufficient to distract the Argentine pilots. The aircraft swept to the north and then turned to run south down the eastern side of the water. Two aircraft, a Mirage and a Skyhawk, came over the hill firing at SIR PERCIVALE. All her guns were firing and as the aircraft banked to run down her starboard side puffs of smoke appeared out their tails. Their bombs, however, landed about 50 yards astern, having passed over the ship. At the vital moment with an aircraft in the sights, the Bofors gun lost all electrical power! Both aircraft left to the south smoking badly, and were finished off by Rapier missiles as they attempted to escape.

SIR PERCIVALE sailed that evening to the Task Group, but just before sunset ATLANTIC CONVEYOR was hit by an Exocet missile.

SIR PERCIVALE was next to ATLANTIC CONVEYOR in the screen and only a couple of miles away, she went in to give assistance picking up and searching for survivors. As she approached ATLANTIC CONVEYOR, which was well alight with a 10/15 foot diameter hole in her port quarter, a frigate went alongside amongst fierce fire and dense smoke to pull liferafts clear. Helicopters flew around searching for survivors and plucking people from the ships bow. It was now dark making the task that much harder.

Back in San Carlos Water SIR PERCIVALE's unloading stopped on Sunday 30 May and she was told she was to take on board PoW's. They began arriving in mid afternoon—being brought out by Sea King. In all she had between 250 and 300 on board on the tank deck. During the night it was suspected that a high level bombing raid was carried out on San Carlos Water, but it achieved no hits or casualties.

Plans were changed yet again and she discharged the PoW's the next day by Mexe-float and commenced priority loading for a trip to Teal Inlet.

The charts indicate a very difficult and dangerous passage through Salvador Water to Teal. It is very narrow and subject to strong tidal effects.

She sailed from San Carlos at 03.30 on Wednesday 2 June and entered Salvador Water at 07.40. The waters had been swept for mines by landing craft from HMS Fearless—using a very makeshift method of a wire with a heavy weight at the end. Exact locations of enemy positions, if any, were not known. The passage was made in darkness. The only noises were from animals on the shore and sporadic Spanish chatter on the VHF. All this time almost 600 troops were on board. She dropped anchor at 08.55 without mishap. She was now very close to the front and discharging much needed equipment in an area that had doubtless never seen such a ship of this size.

Over the next few days SIR PERCIVALE made another run into Teal Inlet with more equipment and ammunition. She carried out a RAS in Teal Inlet with RFA SIR GALAHAD to take on Avcat, and had a very heavy helicopter refuelling task. She refuelled continuously some days and whilst in Teal Inlet refuelled no less than 57 helicopters during the daylight hours of Saturday 5 June.

On Tuesday 8 June—whilst back in San Carlos Water there were more air attacks in Falkland Sound.

After more resupply runs to Teal, Sir Percivale sailed on Monday 16 June to Port Stanley. At 12.30 she entered Port Stanley and at 13.00 dropped anchor to the sound of church bells. She was the first British Ship to enter Port Stanley since the Operation started. At last it was all over . . .

A fine study of the LSL Sir Percivale in San Carlos Water. At one time she was used to house Argentine prisoners taken in the Goose Green battle. So many prisoners were taken that the only immediate protection against the bitter cold of the semi Antarctic winter nights was in the hold of a ship.

# RFA PLUMLEAF—OLD LADY—NEW JOB

PLUMLEAF completed Exercise Springtrain in Gibraltar on April 6 and was preparing for a Far East Deployment with HM Ships BROADSWORD and YARMOUTH when she was instructed to proceed north to conduct Replenishment At Sea trials with SS CANBERRA and MV ELK, two of the ships taken up from trade for the Falklands Emergency.

The trials were carried out successfully although no fuel was passed on this occasion and PLUMLEAF then went on to Portland for last minute stores.

She sailed from Portland on April 19 in company with HM Ships ARDENT, ARGONAUT and RFA REGENT.

PLUMLEAF arrived at Ascension on May 1 and on May 2 carried out the first "live" RAS with SS CANBERRA. She was alongside her for nine hours and issued 2000 tons of fuel. To mark the occasion, the Captain of CANBERRA presented PLUMLEAF with his Commodores burgee which was flown at every subsequent RAS.

PLUMLEAF left Ascension on May 3 after a RAS with HMS FEARLESS and went south to meet up with the LSL Group on May 11 and then proceeded to 50 degrees south where all the ships came together.

After transferring most of her fuel to her sister ship, PEARLEAF, she then returned north—to reload from BRITISH DART—and then south again to meet and fuel the first of the "back up" ships, the BRISTOL group.

PLUMLEAF then established the first of the "Motorway Stations" at 40° south and fuelled ships on their way north and south. At the beginning of June she swopped stations with APPLELEAF and spent two weeks at 25° south. During this period she fuelled the Cable Ship IRIS, RFA FORT AUSTIN and HM Ships GLASGOW, ALACRITY and ARGONAUT.

The end of June brought a change of scene and after a couple of days in Ascension PLUMLEAF was appointed the "Motorway tanker" near the Canary Islands. During this period she fuelled all the ships returning from the Falklands as well as the replacements on the way south including the RANGATIRA carrying the Royal Engineers to rebuild Port Stanley Airfield.

The final RASs were with HMS FEARLESS and HMS INTREPID on July 10 and PLUMLEAF arrived in Gibraltar at 2000 on July 22, just as the World Cup Final was kicking off!

She was then stationed at Gibraltar and RAS'd a further ten ships on their way to and from Ascension.

During the period April 19 to August 26 PLUMLEAF steamed 26,000 miles, issued 20,000 tons of fuel to HM and Merchant ships underway at sea in fifty five separate operations. She received 11,000 tons of fuel from BP tankers. She spent 85 days at sea.

RFA Pearleaf ploughs through a South Atlantic swell. Although nominally a freighting tanker with only a limited replenishment capability she and her sister Plumleaf did sterling service refuelling both warships and merchantmen.

# RMAS TYPHOON

The ocean going tug RMAS TYPHOON is pictured here alongside an LSL at Ascension. TYPHOON left Portland for Ascension on Sunday 4 April and was thus one of the very first ships to sail south—a day ahead of the main Task Force. After spending 12 days at Ascension providing other ships with fresh water she sailed for South Georgia. She spent a month there with civilian salvage tugs attempting to pump out the Argentine submarine SANTA FE. TYPHOON also ferried Gurkhas, Welsh and Scots Guards from QE2 to CANBERRA and NORLAND. Later TYPHOON towed LSL SIR GALAHAD from Bluff Cove out to sea to be sunk as a war grave—and her damaged sister, SIR TRISTRAM, to Port Stanley to be used as an accommodation ship.

# THE MAIL MUST GET THROUGH

Mail from home kept morale high. Considerable efforts were made to deliver letters to the Task Force. These included flying it south from Ascension and air dropping the sacks from RAF Hercules transports into the sea. HMS Active is ready to recover it . . .

Morale back home was also important! Most servicemen wrote regularly to keep their families "in the picture". They also received bundles of "fan mail" from schools and many many youngsters. It seemed half the country wrote letters of support to the men in the South Atlantic . . .

# THE MERCHANT NAVY GOES TO WAR

The Merchant Navy has throughout our nation's history been regarded as a fourth arm of the Services and, true to tradition, their contribution to the Falklands Operation was enthusiastic and loyal. Without it the Falklands would still be in Argentine hands.

The Ministry of Defence requisitioned 54 ships from 33 companies, this made the Ministry one of the world's largest merchant ship operators. More important was the determination, flexibility and bravery of these ships crews. Always ready to do that bit extra and give their best.

## SS CANBERRA

The "Great White Whale"—as CANBERRA was nicknamed—slipped away from Southampton on Good Friday evening as bands played and crowds cheered (and wept) farewell. On her way south to Freetown and Ascension, she "worked up" as a unit of the Fleet.

She was replenished from RFA tankers, operated helicopters once the ad hoc landing pads were completed and conducted a variety of naval exercises which bound her merchant navy crew, embarked naval party and military force into one unit. During this voyage south, her fortnight's halt at Ascension and subsequent passage to the Falklands, the troops on board were subjected to a stream of training exercises—physical fitness, weapon training, lectures, briefings—so at the landing their physical and psychological state had been honed to razor sharpness.

On board was 40 and 42 Commando, Royal Marines and 3rd Battalion, The Parachute Regiment as well as smaller units. A few days before the landings 40 Commando and 3 Para were transferred to the Assault Ships HMS FEARLESS and HMS INTREPID. At dawn on Friday 21 May this luxury liner and the rest of the amphibious fleet steamed into San Carlos Water. She retained 42 Commando—as a reserve for 3 Commando Brigade. They were disembarked later that day.

But then the air raids started, breaking the tranquility of the loch and frightening away the crowds of inquisitive marine birds. All day waves of aircraft skimmed over the hills to fly through streams of red tracer. A bomb splashed into the water 30 feet from CANBERRA's stern, had it exploded her cruising days could have well been over!

That evening all the ships which didn't have to stay in San Carlos Water steamed to the relative safety of the Main Task Force. CANBERRA, having disembarked all her troops, was despatched to South Georgia with NORLAND to meet QE2 and take the troops she had been transporting back to San Carlos Water. It was felt that QE2 could not be sent direct to San Carlos because she would be too attractive a propaganda target for the Argentine Commanders.

Her next job was to embark a host of Argentine prisoners of war from the Islands. CANBERRA was eventually given a guarantee of safe passage to take them to Puerto Madra in southern Argentina for repatriation.

After the surrender CANBERRA embarked most of the Royal Marines of 3 Commando Brigade and sailed for Southampton and the huge emotive welcome as the great white whale returned to her home port. It had been some cruise—unlikely to be on offer in any holiday brochure . . .

SS Canberra about to start replenishing her fuel tanks from RFA Tidepool on the long voyage south from Ascension. Canberra's ad hoc flight decks can be clearly seen.

## NORLAND—WORKHORSE OF THE SOUTH ATLANTIC

NORLAND, the North Sea Ferry, carried men of 2nd Battalion, The Parachute Regiment, to the South Atlantic. They claim to be the first troops to set foot ashore in the amphibious landings, she had five tense days in "Bomb Alley".

While under air attack there the troops remaining on board lined the upper decks with small arms and fired at passing Argentine aircraft. Later she welcomed HMS ANTELOPE's survivors with a signal "Have beds, hot meal and a cool beer for all Antelopes". She then took Gurkhas to the Falklands, POWs to Argentina and stayed in Port Stanley as an accommodation ship. With several trips to Ascension ferrying troops on the first stage of their journey home her crew had been kept far busier than on their normal 24 hour "hops" across the North Sea.

She proved a versatile vessel whose crew adapted to every new task they were asked to perform—many men of the task force have a soft spot for "good old Norland".

# "CROSS DECKING"

Troops of 5 Infantry Brigade being transferred from QE2 to Canberra and smaller ships in Cumberland Bay East, South Georgia on 28 May.

# MV EUROPIC FERRY

The ship was requisitioned on 19 April, for service with the South Atlantic Task Force. During the next three days she was modified at Southampton for her new role, including fitting of replenishment at sea (RAS) equipment, a fresh water evaporator, extra radio and naval communication equipment and additional extra diesel and freshwater tanks. A Royal Naval party was embarked to man communications and generally assist in dealing with the military. The cargo consisted mainly of equipment for 2 Para and 656 Squadron Army Air Corps—Vehicles, 3 Scout helicopters and associated stores, a large quantity of reserve ammunition and general military equipment. Personnel were embarked from these units, with a detachment from the Royal Army Medical Corps.

She sailed from Portland on Sunday 25 to rendezvous with ATLANTIC CONVEYOR off Plymouth that evening, and they sailed in company to Freetown. Topped up with fuel and fresh water she headed for Ascension, arriving on the 7 May.

She sailed that night with the amphibious group including HMS FEARLESS. The whole atmosphere had undergone drastic change, ships were darkened, navigation lights extinguished, radar was not to be used and ships were ordered to keep their assigned station. Fortunately the first few nights under these conditions were moonlit! When "Defence Watches" were instituted the ships company were divided into two watches so that half the crew were up and alert at any time. Personnel remained in their clothing at all times. Glass fittings were taped up to prevent shattering and furniture was securely lashed down. Extra lookouts were posted and the engine room manning increased. During the passage south more ships joined the group.

For her own defence an armament of machine guns and hand held "Blowpipe missiles" were on board.

## D-Day

The group now consisted of five RFA logistic landing ships (LSLs), two RFA supply ships, a strong frigate escort and three merchant ships, namely CANBERRA, NORLAND and EUROPIC FERRY. The principal units of this amphibious force were the assault ships FEARLESS and INTREPID. The weather during this phase of the operation had deteriorated but it gave vital cover. It was well reported on how the Amphibious force navigated through Falkland Sound that night and into San Carlos Water, successfully disembarking troops and equipment before the enemy realised the extent of the operation. Entering San Carlos just before dawn on what promised to be a sunny winter day and seeing CANBERRA lying at anchor epitomised a cruise brochure scene, only it was soon broken by the harsh reality of war as tracer flew through the pale light of dawn over Fanning Head.

EUROPIC FERRY anchored in her allocated position and the sky became alive with helicopters ferrying men and equipment ashore, her first load was the battery of six 105 mm field guns with their ready use ammunition. The sky was now cloudless and gave no cover from air attack. The first indication of impending action was an overall quietness and calm in the anchorage as most helicopters found cover on shore. HMS INTREPID in the next anchorage to EUROPIC FERRY broke the silence by sounding her whistle to alert our forces ashore. In this first attack by Mirage, Skyhawks and Pucara on the beachhead, action was concentrated around the CANBERRA and NORLAND and during this engagement Intrepid brought down a Pucara with a Seacat missile. In subsequent attacks the length of San Carlos Water was overflown—now the LSLs and EUROPIC FERRY became targets. There were some near misses especially one bomb that dropped between her and INTREPID. On these occasions the ship brought its "main armament" of machine guns to bear and whilst claiming no hits she did fire in anger which was a great boost for morale. Throughout the day she continued as an operating deck for helicopters, whilst discharging equipment into landing craft from the stern door.

Her crew altered the ships paint work. Forces ashore at San Carlos had remarked on how distinctive a target her contrasting orange hull and white upper works were so the funnel was painted grey and her outline was broken up with grey paint where possible. This hideous mottled appearance was worthwhile if only one Argentinian pilot was put off making EUROPIC FERRY his target.

On the 25 May she closed with the CANBERRA to embark her Sea King flight for passage to San Carlos.

The following day was spent discharging equipment and ammunition in San Carlos, it was relatively peaceful, although there were a number of air raid warnings only one high level bombing run materialised.

EUROPIC FERRY subsequently returned to the Task Force and two days later sailed to the logistics waiting area which had been established to the east of the Total Exclusion Zone and further away from the threat of air attacks. Here she remained until the 9 June.

Relief was to occur when she met up with HMS BRILLIANT, ST EDMUND and CONTENDER BEZANT. Onboard the latter were Chinook helicopters, which were urgently required ashore. The plan after blading up one aircraft on CONTENDER BEZANT, was to use EUROPIC FERRY's deck to hold the aircraft whilst another was prepared onboard CONTENDER BEZANT—the pair then flying off in company, repeating this operation until all Chinooks had departed. The weather interfered at this point and delayed the initial transfer which resulted in the first aircraft departing on its own. With the second Chinook on deck she was subjected to about 36 hours of continuous force 10 and 11 gales, with a heavy swell up to 50 feet at times. Such was the severity of the storm that on several occasions she was in danger of losing the Chinook over the side. On the morning of the 16 the weather had moderated sufficiently and the Chinook flew off. After a spell in Port Stanley it was time to load stores and retrace steps to Southampton. Life on the cross channel run will never be the same again!

## ELK

The P and O Ferrymasters container ship Elk receives fresh water from HMS Fearless while steaming through the Total Exclusion Zone.

## BRITISH TAMAR

The Assault Ship HMS Intrepid prepares to take on fuel in an "astern RAS" from the civilian tanker British Tamar. Usually RFA oilers went alongside the civilian tankers and took their fuel on board. Later they would transfer this to the warships. The RFAs were better equipped to replenish at sea than the civilian ships. In one operation British Tamar transferred fuel to RFA Pearleaf for a record breaking 54 hours.

# HMS AVENGER

During the conflict HMS AVENGER was on the gun line off the Falklands coast eight times, and fired 1,100 of the 8,000 rounds of 4.5 inch shells expended by the Task Force in naval gunfire support. During the first of these operations HMS AVENGER had the dubious distinction of being the first ship to be attacked by a shore launched missile. It passed harmlessly—just five feet above her flight deck. Later she supported 42 Commando and 2 Para attacking Two Sisters and Mount Longdon, and the Scots Guards in their assault on Tumbledown and Mount William. Using Army spotters, based both ashore and in her Lynx helicopter, HMS AVENGER's gun's accuracy proved capable of destroying single machine gun nests at ranges of 10 miles—in one salvo!

The ship covertly inserted two Royal Marine SBS teams by night. It was very shortly after detaching from the main Task Force for the first of these that HMS AVENGER was attacked simultaneously by four A4 bombers and two Super Etendard aircraft which launched Exocet missiles. Sea Dart missiles from her consort HMS EXETER hit one Super Etendard after missile release and one A4. HMS AVENGER's gun then destroyed one Exocet in flight and one A4, the other missile running wide. The remaining two A4's dropped bombs, which narrowly missed, and then passed very close to the ship's side—below the level of the level of the bridge.

Like her sister ships HMS AVENGER escorted many merchant ships and Royal Fleet Auxiliaries safely in and out of San Carlos Water.

On 15 June HMS AVENGER was in Fox Bay, West Falkland to take the surrender of the Argentine 18th Infantry Regiment and its supporting engineers—some 950 men. This was accomplished, at least initially, with typical British underkill, by the First Lieutentant, one officer and four ratings dropped by helicopter. The weather being too rough for boats to be used.

HMS AVENGER's remaining time in the Falkland's was split between protecting the Carrier Battle Group, acting as Guardship at Port Stanley and San Carlos Water, and giving practical help to isolated communities. On a more grisly note, the ship was able to give a decent burial to the occupants of an Argentine Lear Jet that five weeks earlier the ship's company had watched being shot down over West Falkland by a Sea Dart missile from HMS EXETER.

Time was also found to help construct the permanent memorial to those killed in HMS ARDENT and HMS ANTELOPE.

HMS Avenger shows off her underwater paintwork as she takes on board the hose from the RFA tanker ahead of her — much needed fuel at last . . .

# HMS HERMES

Well out to the east of the Falklands, HMS HERMES had to be kept well out of range of Argentine aircraft—her loss could have been catastrophic and could not be risked.

The contribution made by HMS HERMES was fundamental to British victory. The Sea Harrier aircraft she operated established air superiority. Her Sea King helicopters became maids of all work—anti-submarine, liaison, surface seach, troop carrying, search and rescue, ship transfer, store carrying—the list seems endless . . .

HMS HERMES herself acted in numerous roles throughout the campaign including logistic resupply of ships by helicopter, air co-ordination ship, support ship for the forward operating base on East Falkland and as a mail receipt and distribution centre.

Her story starts in Portsmouth during a period of leave for the ship's company in March. After a hurried recall, they rejoined the ship on 2 April to find her shrouded in scaffolding and covered in dockyard workers preparing her for the unknown days which lay ahead. It is greatly to the credit of Portsmouth Dockyard workforce that she was prepared mechanically and provided with all services needed to get her to sea in record time.

When HMS HERMES (and HMS INVINCIBLE) left Portsmouth on 5 April, the city gave her a tumultuous send-off. With characteristic naval understatement, this was recorded by the bosun's mate in the ship's log as "large crowds wave ship off".

Eight thousand miles later, the flagship entered the Total Exclusion Zone and saw combat with the Argentine occupation force on 1 May with air attacks against Port Stanley and Goose Green airfields. Three weeks of combat were to separate this initial encounter to our forces' landing at San Carlos Bay. During these three weeks the Sea Harrier pilots set about establishing air supremacy over the islands and adjacent sea areas. On 21 May HERMES' pilots claimed 10 Argentine aircraft destroyed. Seven were later confirmed as "kills"—with three probables. Special operations launched by HERMES' Sea King helicopters of 846 Squadron included the special forces attacks on Pebble Island in West Falkland in which 11 light aircraft were destroyed. Air superiority was attained to such an extent that the land forces were able to establish their beachhead without a single man being lost during the landings.

The Argentine Air Force used some of its remaining assets in the attack against Sir Galahad and Sir Tristram at Bluff Cove. A pair of Sea Harriers from HMS HERMES did however destroy four Mirage aircraft during this devastating set back to the advancing troops.

Whilst the Harriers hit the headlines each time they smashed an opposing aircraft—it was the helicopters that had the hard, unsung role. Hour after hour of routine flying—in far from routine circumstances.

In the 3 month period up to HERMES' withdrawal from the Falkland Islands area, 826 Squadron kept their Sea King Mk 5 helicopters airborne around the clock. In May one helicopter from the squadron was actually airborne for a third of the month.

Not a single Sea Harrier was lost in air combat, although four were brought down by ground fire. Two pilots were killed. Units embarked in the flagship claimed 46 aircraft destroyed of which 39 were listed as confirmed "kills".

HMS HERMES' last major attack was a dawn strike against Stanley airfield on 8 June when a quartet of Sea Harriers tossed bombs from three miles' range into the middle of a "pink glowing dome" of anti-aircraft fire-punctuated by the tracks of surface-to-air missiles, all of which were avoided. At the end of the conflict, the Sea Harriers from HMS HERMES had flown more than 1,000 missions.

On 3 July HERMES entered Port William Sound, just north of Stanley, 28 aircraft were launched for a "victorious fly-past" over Port Stanley.

HMS Hermes displays most of her air group on deck. Her ships side tells its own story . . .

## The Silent Service . . .

The activities of the submarines in the South Atlantic were shouded in secrecy. Their ability to undertake these patrols kept the entire Argentine Fleet in local waters. A major relief to the Task Force Commanders. The Argentine Air Force was a large enough headache—surface ships could have only made matters worse .

HMS Conqueror returning home to Faslane after 90 days on patrol—the longest ever by a Royal Naval Submarine. Her engagement with the Argentine Cruiser General Balgrano is believed to be the most southerly naval battle and certainly the first involving a nuclear submarine.

The only conventional submarine to make the long haul south was HMS Onyx. Her main role was to slip men of the SAS and SBS ashore—behind enemy lines. Advance intelligence from these special forces was vital to the planning staff. Their story may never be told . . .

Another nuclear submarine—HMS Valiant—in company with the frigate HMS Penelope.
Very little time was spent above the surface by these submarines. All the time they were beneath the waves it was pure guesswork where they were—and what they were doing. Onboard it was more of a problem on how to fill the long, lonely, days . . .

# HMS PENELOPE

The passage south was fast and the ship successfully negotiated everything from intensive weapons training to the perils of King Neptune's Court. The 18th May found PENELOPE at Ascension Island, anchored just long enough to embark last minute stores, ammunition and mail.

A Boeing 707 aircraft provided the first encounter with the enemy on 22 May when the long range reconnaissance aircraft appeared on the radar screens and 'Action Stations' was sounded in anger for the first time. The aircraft was engaged by Sea Dart missiles from HMS BRISTOL and HMS CARDIFF but they were fired at extreme range and the Boeing escaped.

By 25 May the effects of a South Atlantic winter began to be felt. The temperature had dropped dramatically. No steam heating in the ship though—a ploy which successfully encouraged all to wear 3 or 4 layers of warm clothing. Refuelling at sea became a more hazardous evolution as the seas roughened. News of the loss of HMS COVENTRY and ATLANTIC CONVEYOR reached the ship, and provoked an atmosphere of shock, anger and resolution.

Sonar contacts became more frequent over the next few days, mostly caused by marine life and ship's wakes. It was a sad aspect of the anti-submarine measures taken by some ships, that South Atlantic whales frequently suffered the devastating effects of torpedo and depth charge attacks.

The carrier battle group appeared on the horizon early on the morning of 27 May. At lunchtime, the ship went to action stations, in response to our first 'Air Raid Warning Red' in the Total Exclusion Zone. Fortunately the only casualty was lunch!

Later PENELOPE was detached from the Battle Group with HMS MINERVA towards East Falkland. The main task was to escort our damaged sister ship HMS ARGONAUT out of San Carlos Water.

Returning to the carrier group on 30 May PENELOPE's Lynx helicopter departed to HMS HERMES as an air raid developed. Enemy aircraft attacked the force, and one, a Super Etendard probably fired an Exocet. One of the accompanying aircraft was shot down as it attempted to bomb a Type 21 frigate. Later in the day another air raid warning was called but the raid didn't develop. Subsequently, the Argentinian Junta claimed to have hit HMS INVINCIBLE during these raids!

HMS PENELOPE adopted the role of Battle Group post box on 1 and 2 June; detached for air drops she sailed to the north east of the Falklands to rendezvous with an RAF Hercules aircraft from Ascension Island. These Hercules provided an air ferry for essential stores to the Task Force. As well as the stores, she also collected from the sea the new Commanding Officer of 2nd Para Lt. Col. David Chaundler who parachuted in from 1500 feet. The ship's company were disappointed when the Colonel's dog failed to arrive in the next drop!

Back with the battle group on 3 June, life involved going round in ever decreasing circles. Once again stores were despatched, the ship refuelled and the weather continued to be unfriendly. However, life in the Task Force was always unpredictable and PENELOPE was detached for 3 days in San Carlos Water.

She slipped quietly into the loch just after daybreak on 4 June, and started what was to be the routine for the next 13 days—not the 3 days planned. From sunrise to dusk the days were spent at full action stations and the nights at defence stations usually escorting fast convoys of troops and supply ships to and from San Carlos Water. There were frequent 'Red Alerts', and it became clear the Argentinians were making a determined effort to blitz San Carlos and the precious supply chain of merchant ships. Food was rudimentary and had to be nibbled fast at the place of action: such delights as Bamps (Bomb Alley Meat Pies) and tinned sausages kept the ship's company going.

When at action stations in San Carlos Water, and under direct threat of air attack, the helicopter would automatically be launched and fly towards land to hover until the attack was over. This tactic avoided damage to a valuable asset and achieved instant Search and Rescue readiness should the ship have been hit. On the night of 9 June the ship sailed to one of the northern islands in the West Falklands for clandestine operations, and slipped quietly back into San Carlos at dawn. During these nights around the Falklands much evidence of the artillery action and fierce fighting ashore was seen—with the sky continually illuminated by flares and gunfire. The 10th June also saw a particularly high incidence of 'red warnings' as the Argentinian Air Force once again turned their attention to San Carlos. Good warning and good combat air patrol cover by Sea Harriers, kept them at bay.

Early on 14 June several enemy aircraft, including Exocet carrying Super Etendards, attacked our troops surrounding Stanley and harrassed British shipping. As they opened to the north east they spotted PENELOPE with a merchantman in company. A missile was launched from the air and most of those on the upper deck saw its menacing red glow as it descended from the launch aircraft and skimmed at wavetop height towards the ship.

The ship avoided the missile by violent high speed manoeuvring. It was a most sobering experience. The merchantman, unaware of the dire danger, observed PENELOPE's dramatic missile firing actions and signalled "I enjoyed the firework display".

News of the first Argentinian surrender came in later that day PENELOPE thus claimed to be the last ship to come under air attack during the Falkland Operation.

The following week was spent at Ports William and Stanley. In this relatively quiet period the ship was able to send parties of the ship's company ashore to view Stanley. The scars of war were most apparent and the sheer volume of Argentinian ammunition and equipment surprised everybody.

## HMS ARGONAUT

Arriving at Falkland Sound on 20 May, HMS ARGONAUT was part of the escort which brought in the amphibious ships. Once they had anchored and the landing began, she took up her station at the entrance to San Carlos as part of the anti-aircraft defence of the Force.

The first attack came when an Argentine reconnassiance aircraft came over the hills firing rockets and cannon. ARGONAUT suffered slight damage and three men were wounded. This was the start of frequent attacks by many Argentinian aircraft that went on throughout the day. The ship fired Seacat missiles, bofors shells and much small arms ammunition, and accounted for one aircraft and one "shared". The enemy pressed home attacks on the frigates and destroyers determindly, his losses were severe, but the amphibious ships, merchant vessels and landing beaches were untouched.

In the afternoon the attacks intensified and ARGONAUT found herself receiving the undivided attention of Six Skyhawk fighter bombers. Although one of these was destroyed and others probably hit, two attacks were successful. An observer in HMS FEARLESS said that ARGONAUT disappeared behind a curtain of bomb splashes.

The ship was hit twice by 1,000 lb bombs. One entered the boiler room where it caused small fires and substantial damage to machinery and brought both engines to a halt, but failed to explode. The other entered the ship below the waterline forward, passed through a fuel tank and destroyed much of the forward magazine, where it caused a number of explosions of ship's ammunition, but itself failed to explode. Two seamen were killed in this attack.

Despite this damage, which could have been much worse, most weapon systems were still functioning, and the ship continued, at anchor, to fight on until nightfall when the attacks ceased for that day.

Meanwhile the damage control teams had extinguished fires, started pumps, and effected some emergency repairs. HMS PLYMOUTH gave much support and eventually towed ARGONAUT into San Carlos Water with the landing ships.

During the next eight days ARGONAUT continued the fight in "Bomb Alley" under the constant threat of attack by day. While several ships were hit ARGONAUT escaped further damage and claimed two more aircraft. During this period the two bombs, which were in a dangerous condition, were removed, repairs to machiney progressed and the ship made watertight.

On 30 May ARGONAUT sailed to rendezvous with a repair ship for further repairs. Subsequently she operated with the main battle group for two days before being detached to UK.

Forty years ago in the Mediterranean the previous ARGONAUT suffered severe damager when she was also hit by enemy action, but in a classic damage-control operation was able to restore watertight integrity and some machinery, and eventually made a friendly port. As Jason will remember, the ARGONAUTS usually win through.


## HMS INVINCIBLE

HMS INVINCIBLE spent 166 days at sea, believed to be the longest period of continous carrier operations ever—nearly two weeks longer than the previous record of 153 days by the USS EISENHOWER. It was a period of intense professional and personal challenge for the 1000 strong ship's company.

INVINCIBLE deployed with the Task Force on 5 April and her subsequent employment went through several distinct phases—demonstrating the inherent flexibility of sea power and the versatility of the INVINCIBLE class aircraft carriers and their air group of Sea Harriers and Sea Kings. In the first phase of the deployment INVINCIBLE was part of the main Task Force whose progress south was watched with intense interest around the world—particularly in Argentina!

The sailing of the Task Force made British determination quite clear and backed up the political pressure being brought to bear on Argentina. When the presence of the Task Force and political efforts failed to achieve their objective, the Task Force entered the Total Exclusion Zone, and action commenced to regain the Islands by military means. In this phase the Sea Harriers of 801 Squadron flew combat air patrols over the Falklands shooting down 7 enemy aircraft, with 3 more "probables" claimed. Only 12 Sidewinder missiles were used to achieve this.

The Sea Harriers lived up to their excellent reputation, claiming a steadily increasing toll of Argentine aeroplanes, without losing a single one of their number in air to air combat.

Tragically two pilots were lost with their aircraft in what appears to have been a mid-air collision in very poor weather. Another aircraft was lost to a surface to air missile, though the pilot was recovered by helicopter after an eight hour search and rescue mission close to the enemy coast.

The Sea Kings of 820 Squadron provided anti-submarine protection for the Force, and flew a number of other missions supporting ground forces ashore. The success of the anti-submarine screen provided by the Sea Kings must be judged by the fact that there was not a single submarine attack on any ship of the Force.

Once the Islands were regained INVINCIBLE entered the third phase of the deployment, in many ways the most taxing, with a long period providing a deterrent presence off the Islands. After HERMES sailed for the UK on 5 July, INVINCIBLE shared this air duty, with the RAF Harrier Squadron based at Stanley. INVINCIBLE sailed for the UK on 29 July after handing over to her sister ship, HMS ILLUSTRIOUS.

The announcement that INVINCIBLE was to be retained in the Royal Navy and not sold to the Royal Australian Navy was the best possible news received onboard during the deployment and a vindication of the view long expressed by the Navy that three carriers were essential in the Fleet—if two were always to be available.

## HMS INVINCIBLE—THE FACTS

166 continuous days at sea—a world record for continuous aircraft carrier operations. Miles steamed 51,660 (twice around the world).

The fuel (diesel) consumed (30,196 tonnes) would be sufficient for a Mini travelling at 40 mpg for a return trip to the sun and on completion 4,000 journeys around the equator.

The aviation fuel consumed (7,620 tonnes) would be sufficient for a Sea Harrier flying at 400 mph to travel to the moon and back—4 times!

Fresh water distilled from the sea—8.6 million gallons. Enough to fill 45 Olympic swimming pools.

Two gas turbine main engines were changed while at sea. No ship had ever attempted to change a gas turbine main engine at sea before.

Engine hours—total of 8011.          Lubricating oil consumed—18,800 gallons.

### Ships' embarked Aircraft Squadron

#### 820 Squadron (Sea King)

| | |
|---|---|
| Hours flown | 4700 |
| Aircraft | 9 |
| Sorties flown | 1650 |
| Each pilots' average hours | 321 |
| Observers average hours | 336 |
| Aircraft average hours | 522 |
| Loads lifted | 1172 |
| Tons of stores lifted | 1200 |
| Torpedoes dropped | 6 |
| Depth charges dropped | 10 |

#### 801 Squadron; (Sea Harriers)

| | |
|---|---|
| Sorties flown | 1430 |
| Types: Fighter | 950 |
| Recce | 180 |
| Bomb/Strike | 300 |
| Flying Hours | 1580 |
| Aircraft | 8 |
| Hours per pilot | 122 |
| Kills | 7 |
| Probables | 3 |
| Sidewinders fired | 12 |
| Bombs | 56 |

30mm fired 2000 rounds
Average combat sorties per pilot 57
Average combat hours per pilot 73
(This was 3x normal flying rate)
Longest sortie 1 hour 45 minutes
Shortest sortie 10 minutes
Least amount of fuel on recovery 300 lbs
(Fuel needed to fly one minute 300 lbs)
Longest time spent by a pilot in cockpit in one day—9 hours
Quickest scramble—2 mins 35 secs.

### Victuals

Average number victualled 1050 per day
153,168 Eggs
4½ miles (i.e. 70,224) Sausages
282,200 Rolls
19,920 Loaves
108,000 Buns
86 tons of potatoes
301,920 pints of tea
730,400 meals served
Ship's company spent over £¼ millon at the NAFFI. They ate ½ million bars of "nutty" (chocolate) and drank 180,000 drinks from the vending machines.

### The War

45 days at war
263 hours at Action Stations
Miles steamed 15,299
15% of time spent in fog. 31% of time in sea state 5 or greater.
6 Sea Dart missiles were fired in anger on 25 May in less than 2 minutes—believed to be the greatest number of missiles fired by an RN ship in such a short time.

## HMS GLAMORGAN—A Falklands Diary

| 1 May | —Detached with ARROW & ALACRITY to bombard Stanley. |
| | 1940 —Four Argentinian Mirage attack ships. One shot down over Stanley by Argentinian army! Two 500lb bombs dropped on GLAMORGAN resulting in two near misses either side of the quarterdeck. Minor underwater damage subsequently found, but no effect on propulsion or fighting ability. Retire from gun line until after dark. |
| | 2240 —Return to gun line. |
| 2 May | 0150 —Complete bombardment (which attracted counter battery fire from shore). |
| 6 May | —GLAMORGAN, ARROW & ALACRITY detached as Surface Action Group to investigate possible surface contact in vicinity of SHEFFIELD hulk. (False alarm, contact identified as friendly helicopter). |

The SAS arrive. The tug Irishman stands by to assist Glamorgan with their recovery.

| 14 May | 2000 —Detached to bombard Pebble Island in support of the SAS. |
| 15 May | 0400 —On Pebble Island gun line. |
| | 0745 —Bombardment complete. Retire at 29 knots (down sea) in force 9 conditions. 14 aircraft destroyed in this highly successful combined operation. |
| 16 May | 1830 —Detached to bombard targets between Stanley and Lively Island. |
| 18 May | 1800 —Detached to bombard as part of the landing deception plan. |
| 19 May | 0400 —Start bombardment between Lively Island and Stanley. |
| | 1800 —Detach to bombard Bertha's Beach. |
| 20 May | 0250 —Bertha's Beach and targets around Stanley bombarded drawing the usual counter battery fire. Over 600 rounds fired to date. |
| | 2000 —Detach to bombard north of Berkeley Sound. Aim was to make as much noise as possible to draw attention away from San Carlos Water. |
| 21 May | 0200 —Start bombardment in Berkeley Sound area. |
| | 0400 —Complete bombardments. |
| | 0630 'H' Hour in San Carlos Water. |
| 25 May | 1940 —Under Exocet attack. |
| | 1943 —ATLANTIC CONVEYOR hit by Exocet. |
| | 2130 —Detached to bombard Stanley area (as a reprisal for the Exocet raid). |
| 26 May | 0345 —Started bombardments, drawing considerable counter battery fire. |
| 27 May | 2015 —Detach with ALACRITY & AVENGER to bombard Stanley area. |
| 28 May | 0230 —Start bombardments. Attract 155mm Howitzer counter battery fire. |
| | 0510 —Bombardment complete. |
| 29 May | 1830 —Detach to Stanley gun line. |
| 30 May | 0315 —On gun line ready for calls for fire in support of troops on Mount Kent. Aircraft at Stanley airport also engaged. |
| | 0355 —30 rounds fired at 155mm Howitzers on Sapper Hill in support of AMBUSCADE who was under heavy fire. |
| | 0730 —Bombardments complete. |
| | 1735 —Under Exocet attack (unsuccessful). Detach on completion to the Tug Repair and Logistics Area (TRALA). |
| 30 May-<br>11 June | —TRALA Manager, controlling the support ships and collecting airdrop stores from RAF Hercules. |
| 11 June | 1700 —Detach at 26 knots to support 45 Commando on Two Sisters. YARMOUTH in company. |
| 12 June | 0001 —On the gun line. |
| | 0615 —Bombardments completed. |

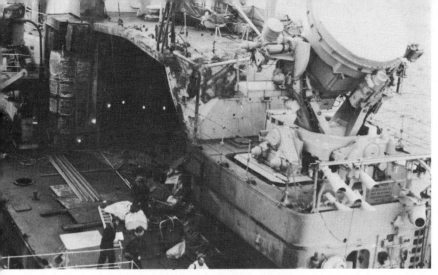

Glamorgan battle damage after surviving Exocet hit.

| | | |
|---|---|---|
| 12 June | 0636 | Exocet land based missile detected on radar—closing. |
| (cont) | 0637 | —Hit by Exocet missile. Hole blown in upper deck. Hangar and helicopter destroyed. Fires and flooding below in galley and elsewhere cause damage and 10° list, but ship never loses way. 13 killed, 14 wounded. |
| | 1000 | —Proceeding in excess of 20 knots with all fires out, floods pumped. |
| | 1935 | —13 dead buried at sea. All wounded were transferred to HERMES & INVINCIBLE. |
| 13 June | | —Alongside STENA SEASPREAD for repairs. |
| 15 June | | —Storm force winds all day. Wessex helicopter borrowed from TIDESPRING badly damaged by weather on flight deck. |
| 16 June | | —Wind moderated to 25 knots. Succeeded in re-fuelling after 6 hours. Sea moderating slowly. |
| 17 June | | —Continue repairs. |
| | 2330 | —Detached with ACTIVE and STENA SEASPEAD to San Carlos Water. |
| 19 June | 2200 | —Repairs completed—sail from San Carlos Water. |
| 21 June | 1345 | —Take departure from Force firing full calibre salute on passing close to HERMES. A total of 1243 rounds fired during whole operation—more than any other ship. PLYMOUTH in company. |
| 5 July | | —Complete final (and 54th) RAS. |
| 10 July | | —Return to Portsmouth having steamed over 30,000 miles since being diverted on 2 April. |

## HMS BROADSWORD

BROADSWORD's major brush with the enemy was from 21 to 26 May when she was assigned as the escort commander for the Amphibious Task Group. BROADSWORD's job was to escort them through the Total Exclusion Zone into San Carlos Water.

As well as the redoubtable Seawolf, which claimed one victim on the first day's air raids and a second in Bomb Alley, BROADSWORD had a secret weapon. This was an upper deck small arms battery, a mixed crew of sailors and marines firing machine guns, rifles and 40mm Bofors gun. This team, led by Sergeant Bill Leslie, was a fearsome sight to attacking aircraft, shooting down two of them and damaging two others; despite being strafed by cannon and machine gun fire. One young man who had a lucky escape was Seaman Operator ('Oscar') Whild, aged 21, who joined BROADSWORD for his first sea experience just before she sailed for what he expected to be a trip to the Far East. He was on the upper deck as part of the small arms battery when shrapnel from attacking aircraft ripped his clothing. Apart from being a bit bruised he escaped unhurt and later went on to gain a well earned reputation as a cool customer under fire.

HMS Broadsword's 'extra' air defence team — her secret weapon!

HMS Broadsword battles with the heavy South Atlantic seas.

For five days BROADSWORD was in the thick of the fighting—on 25th May she was operating in company with COVENTRY just North of Pebble Island when 4 aircraft attacked the two ships. In the first wave of two aircraft a bomb dropped just short of BROADSWORD bounced off the sea, crashed through the ships side, out through the upper deck and fell in the sea on the other side of the ship before exploding. In the next wave COVENTRY was not so lucky, she was hit by a 1000lb bomb and was later abandoned. BROADSWORD stopped, lowered all boats and, with the help of helicopters from ashore, set about the harrowing task of recovering survivors. In all over 170 COVENTRY survivors were recovered to BROADSWORD who then made her way into San Carlos Water to transfer them to an RFA for the start of their journey home. As they left the ship in a landing craft the COVENTRY sailors raised three cheers for the ship's company of BROADSWORD in gratitude for their rescue.

The next day BROADSWORD was ordered out of "Bomb Alley" to rejoin the carrier task group operating to the east of the Falklands. She had been lucky; of the nine escorts that experienced Bomb Alley, 3 were sunk, 2 departed with bomb or cannon shell damage after the first day, 1 was laid up with 2 unexploded bombs onboard and only 2 were unscathed. Although pockmarked from cannon shell holes BROADSWORD was able to carry on with her operational task of escorting HERMES.

The bomb bounced off the sea — in through the ships side — up through the flight deck . . .

Leaving behind a very sorry looking Lynx.

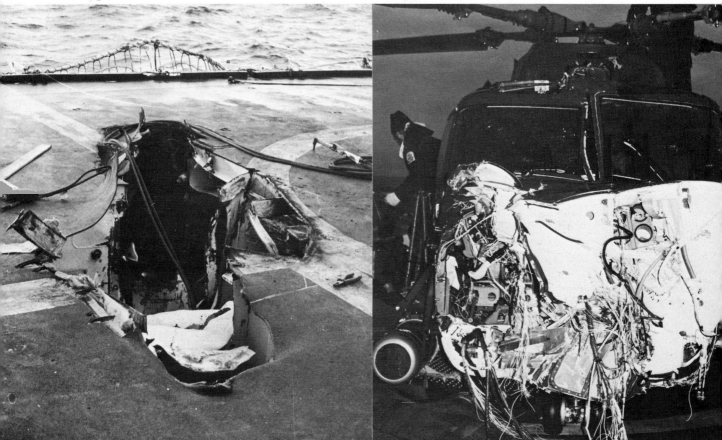

# HMS BRILLIANT

HMS BROADSWORD's sister HMS BRILLIANT also had an eventful war . . .

Highlights of the ships deployment noted from her log read as follows . . .

| Date | | Remarks |
|------|------|---------|
| 14 April | BRILLIANT ordered to take a force of ships into the South Atlantic to act as a 'spearhead group'. | HM ships BRILLIANT, SHEFFIELD COVENTRY, GLASGOW and ARROW. |
| 22 April | Well into South Atlantic — BRILLIANT ordered to proceed to South Georgia. | Weather terrible. |
| 24 April | Joined ANTRIM, PLYMOUTH and ENDURANCE for South Georgia operation. | BRILLIANT's two Lynx helicopters involved in attack on Argentine submarine SANTA FE and landing of troops. |
| 1 May | BRILLIANT detached in charge of anti-submarine force and operated off coast of East Falkland for first time. | First Argentine air attacks on RN ships. |
| 12 May | Whilst operating close off shore HM Ships BRILLIANT and GLASGOW attacked by A4 Skyhawk fighter bombers. | BRILLIANT engages with Sea Wolf missile system — three Skyhawks splashed. GLASGOW gets a bomb through her. Three bombs bounce over BRILLIANT. |
| 15 May | BRILLIANT Lynx fired on whilst operating in South Falkland Sound. | |
| 16 May | BRILLIANT and ALACRITY sweep North Coast and Falkland Sound. | |
| 19 May | Helicopter ditches with SAS troops embarked. | BRILLIANT recovers 8 men, 21 die. |
| 21 May | D—Day. BRILLIANT operates with other ships in Falkland Sound. | ANTRIM, ARGONAUT, BRILLIANT all suffer action damage. |
| | BRILLIANT takes over control of the defending Sea Harriers and vectors them on to many successful engagements. | |
| 25 May | Argentina's National Day — massed air attacks on ships. | Sister ship BROADSWORD hit. COVENTRY sunk. |
| | Super Etendard Exocet attack. Missiles in flight observed from BRILLIANT's Bridge. | ATLANTIC CONVEYOR sunk BRILLIANT recovers 24 survivors. |

Battered—but not beaten—HMS Brilliant returns from the Falklands 13 July 1982.

HMS Leeds Castle.

# "WELLS FARGO" OF THE SOUTH ATLANTIC . . .

## HMS LEEDS CASTLE

The following "blow by blow" account from HMS LEEDS CASTLE makes fascinating reading. The smallest warship of the Task Force reports . . .

April 2   Just back from Easter leave at Portsmouth. Ship'sCompany marched down Fountain Lake Jetty to witness departure of HERMES. An emotional moment. HERMES lying very deep in the water. Dockyard clearly very proud of their amazing 4 day effort.

15-21   A week of beautiful weather in North Sea. Several Trawler boardings. Much fresh fish!

22   Arrived Newcastle for 48 hour stand off. Telephone call from Captain, Fishery Protection. Return to Rosyth forthwith. Why?

23   Arrived Rosyth. FALKLANDS Despatch Vessel is to be our new rôle . . .

24-25   Embarked 50 tons food. Extra 160 tons water, 200 tons fuel. Range now approx 8000 miles at full power. All defects cleared.

27-28   At Portsmouth. Fitted with desalination plant and extra radio equipment amongst other items. War stores embarked.

29   Sailed for Portland. More last minute stores. Flying exercises to remove cobwebs!
     P.M. Sailed for Ascension—3750 miles to go!

May 2   Argentine Cruiser BELGRANO torpedoed. A dangerous air of "EASY" prevails. Continue apace with Weapon/Damage control/Medical/Recognition training.

4   SHEFFIELD ABANDONED. You can hear a pin drop for many minutes. This does more than anything else to make us all aware of the reality of this voyage South. Training suddenly take on a new emphasis. Ship ploughing along happily at 17½ knots. Some mechanical defects rectified.

6   We hear 2 Harriers are lost in a collision. To Defence watches to prove long term organisation. We are suddenly getting quite sharp! Flight Deck sports in the evening—great entertainment.

8   Crossed the equator. Appropriate ceremony in blissful weather. Buffer (Chief Bosun's Mate) makes ugliest Queen on record. A good day.

9   Arrived Ascension. Unloaded 50 tons food in 8 hours. Had estimated it would take 24. Many sore muscles.

10   50 helo loads of vital spares/mail flown on board. Most stored below. Some lashed on Flight Deck.

11   Rosyth Minesweeping trawlers chug into Ascension. Secure stern to volcanic rubble to fuel from BBC generator fuel stocks! Slow process. On completion close pass of trawlers and depart for rendezvous Battle Group (CVBG) in Total Exclusion Zone (TEZ). Russian intelligence gatherer tries to close but hasn't the legs. Final helo loads flown out. Problems with the gun. Reduced to files and hammers to fix it! What would the staff say? After many firings, days and night, Bofors and machine gunners have become extremely fast and accurate.

13   Last day of peace for us—and of sunshine. Flight Deck sports day to celebrate.

15   Camshaft shears. One engine dead.

| May | 16 | Defence watches on permanent basis. Weather deteriorating. Dawn action stations daily. |
|---|---|---|

May 16 Defence watches on permanent basis. Weather deteriorating. Dawn action stations daily.

18 RAF Hercules arrives and parachutes 4 loads. Includes new camshaft. Mail R/V with tanker BRITISH ESK returning with SHEFFIELD survivors. Pipe salute to SHEFFIELD.

20 0300. After 36 hours continuous effort by Engineers the main engine is back on line. 17½ knots again. EXETER/ANTELOPE/AMBUSCADE are some distance behind trying to catch. Unsuccessfully!

21 Arrived in TEZ. Beautiful weather but cold. Amphibious landing begins at Port San Carlos. Air raid warning RED. (Air attack imminent). To ACTION STATIONS. Don't know where carrier group is—but we are looking (earnestly). Friendly Lynx spots us and directs us (not before throwing his notebook into the water to test our searider dinghy reaction!) Listen with horror to airbattle in San Carlos. ARDENT sunk, BROADSWORD/ANTRIM/ARGONAUT damaged. 17 Argentine A/C downed. Most relieved to find Carrier Battle Group at 2300. Given sector on screen. 18 ships in group. Carrying out zig zag. Darkened, radar off.

22 1100—1500 transfer all stores by helo to REGENT.
1530—refuelled from OLMEDA. 3 hours. Well handled by all seamen. Back on screen overnight (Directly up threat!) Not fun on screen without lights or radar. Turned on radar for quick station check to find contact at ½ mile closing! Fog not helping. Missed by 600 yards.

23 Detached to pass mail to REGENT. Steam 100 miles. Pass mail. On recovering searider—"Man Overboard." Sea water is only +5 C. Worst moment to date. Recovered—bit frightened and very cold—Able Seaman Hughes. Recalled to Carrier Group to collect outgoing stores/mail. Back on screen same old sector! ANTELOPE badly damaged at San Carlos. After only 24 hours in TEZ she is lost.

24 On screen. Vertrep urgently needed LUBOIL. Heaving line transfer with ANTRIM. Shell holes in side plugged with wood! Detached again. Night boat transfer to Tug SALVAGEMAN, then CANBERRA. Foggy. See CANBERRA lights at 300 yards. Mail passed. Not the most relaxed way to do things.

25 REGENT again. Still dark very foggy. Lose searider in fog — twice. REGENT apparently unwilling to show a light. Chicken out and abort. To STENA SEASPREAD. With her very sophisticated manoeuvring equipment she comes alongside us and cranes off stores. Assists with Gyro problems. ANTRIM t'other side having shell holes patched up by the man over side in bosun chair with welding equipment. This is all amazing! ATLANTIC CONVEYOR hit by two Exocet. We lay directly between her and the aircraft while on the screen. Sighs of disbelief all round! Night R/V with BRITISH TRENT to pass mail. Our fish VHF DF radio finds her.

26 Chasing CANBERRA to South Georgia. CONVENTRY sunk. Listened to Captain of BROADSWORD calling for air cover and rescue assistance. Another harrowing moment. Signal Traffic remains very heavy. Communicators have been in two watches since leaving. Great difficulty clearing ship/shore radio traffic. Only with perseverance and great help of Canadians at Halifax do we manage.

27 Arrive South Georgia to find CANBERRA. QE II and NORLAND arrive shortly afterwards. Invited to try and lie alongside QE II under her flare to make use of her foscle cranes. Too much flare and slight swell. Damage two aerials in the attempt.

28 Spend day between ships witnessing the amazing spectacle of cross decking 3000 troops. Rosyth trawlers doing superb job (understandably removing Royal Blue paint in the process!). Act as petrol station for the Sea Kings non-stop cross decking stores/vehicles. P.M. Alongside CANBERRA to move ARDENT survivors to QE II. All troops plus band give them a very emotional send off. They are clearly very sad. Lots of plastic bags of belongings.

29 ENDURANCE Wasp helicopter stuck in bay around the corner, in fog. Go round to recover and return to "mum" at Grytviken. Thence away. Cross decking complete. Apart from anything else South Georgia is beautiful — Ice flows/snow/Glaciers everywhere. Spend whole day northbound weaving in amongst beautiful icebergs. One a mile long. When clear — full speed — Ascension bound. Relax to cruising state. Out of range of Argentine aircraft. Hear that troops take Goose Green/Darwin.

31 Argentine Hercules within 180 mile range bombs a tanker. We are within 180 miles! Back to defence stations! Weather terrible — 3 days of rolling up to 35 degrees in heavy quarter sea. Having continuously provided excellent grub — galley succumb to weather and we get first pot mess of the deployment. Not a bad record.

June 6 Arrive Ascension. Detailed as Guardship! ugh! Spend next three weeks there. Sport, Nimrod flights and Helicopter trips around the Island for Ship's company. Banyan barbeques. RAF clamour for our bread and occasionally send helicopter to collect! Give several "around the island" trips for the Army/Navy/RAF who have little fun ashore. Good diving and fishing. Weather compensates for boredom. Both seariders active all day long helping out stream of ships passing through. Damaged Warriors passing through northbound.

14 Argentinian Surrender at Port Stanley. A good day.

| June 22 | Splice the Mainbrace for Prince William. Another good day! |
|---|---|
| 29 | Alongside OLWEN to refuel. Puncture her fender. Nasty metal grating sounds up forward. Leave at the rush. Alongside ALVEGA better fenders and good company. Stored up by helicopter. Mountain of gear on the Flight deck. More below. DUMBARTON CASTLE arrives. Sail for Falklands again. |
| July 5 | R/V with SIR PERCIVALE, going home-having been in the thick of it. Searider mail transfer. |
| 6 | R/V TIDESPRING. Searider mail transfer. |
| 7 | R/V HERMES/BROADSWORD. Foul weather. Only her helicopter seen. |
| 8 | R/V APPLELEAF. Searider transfer. Conditions marginal (very) but they haven't received mail for a long time and send sad signal "please try". As usual seariders performs excellently. |
| 9 | R/V EXETER/CARDIFF/YARMOUTH. They think we can do 20 knots so formation none too neat. |
| 11 | R/V with Carrier Group. Take close station on FORT GRANGE and start Helicopter replenishment. Wind wrong. Put on screen. PM—try again! After 10 loads Sea King ditches in sea on Port bow (close). She floats away. Searider recover crew. FORT GRANGE boat appears, attempts to attach line to helo and capsizes. Searider collects a further 4 passengers. All ships on screen scream onto the scene. More danger of being run down by INVINCIBLE and 4 frigates than anything else! Attempt to tow capsized lifeboat to GRANGE. Tow parts. Now dark. Both seariders have been out for some time and crew are cold. Grange manoeuvrs to drift down onto boat. Seariders spend an hour getting slings onto boat. Boat eventually recovered but damaged. Grange most grateful for excellent work of sea riders. Helo lost. Seariders pick up liferafts and floating debris. Detached to Port Stanley. |
| 12 | Arrive Stanley to offload. Good to see Rosyth Trawlers again. They have done sterling and dangerous work. No helicopters or boats available so both Seariders at it all day long. Alongside MV WALKER—refuel. Alongside REGENT to offload 3 ton gun barrels. Offload not completed but can't hang around so sail for Port San Carlos. |
| 13 | At Port San Carlos more peaceful and organised. Ground snow covered and beautiful in sunshine. Alongside STENA SEASPREAD. Offload. Ship's Company Walk ashore to see memorial to ARDENT/ANTELOPE. Entertain Scots Guards detachement who are living in severe conditions on the beach. Come for shower and bring their washing. Give them 100 camp beds! Anchor overnight. Argie supply ship BUENO (un) SUCCESSO looking forlorn—Damaged by Harriers. |
| 14 | Back alongside STENA SEASPREAD Embark stores. P.M. Sail for Stanley. STENA S an amazing ship can build/repair anything. |
| 15 | Back to Port Stanley alongside GEESTPORT and AVELONA STAR to get rid of the last d....d gun barrel and embark stores for South Georgia, then anchor in inner harbour. Still no sign of Chinook to lift off heavy loads. Gale. Ships dragging all round. Searider rescues APOLLO's Gemini from beach. Their seaboat tried but beached and holed. |
| 16 | Gale again. Searider rescues BRITISH ENTERPRISE III's Gemini off beach. Boats busy as usual all day—usually doing favours for merchant ships who have no "easy to use" boats. Searider tries to rescue huge Yokshama fender but not quite up to it. Approx 15 ships waiting to offload. Tempers a bit frayed. Queens Harbour Master (QHM) with no assets and little cooperation. Air raid warning yellow—to defence stations—contact to west of Falklands. Goes away. Believe it or not our anchorage furthest up threat-again! |
| 17 | Still waiting. Can it be? Yes—a Chinook. We offload and then embark enormous pile for South Georgia. Invited to transfer one of our seariders to FORT GRANGE to replace their damaged boat. This hurts. Chippy works through the night to rectify faults. Weather still miserable. Big ships have to sail to avoid dragging their anchors. |
| 18 | Church party. Stanley is a dreadful dirty mess. Battered Argy Helos and equipment scattered everywhere. P.M. sail alongside AVELONA STAR to collect cabbage etc (4 tons) for INVINCIBLE and finally away after what should have been 12 hours in Stanley! (but was 3 days). |
| 19 | R/V with INVINCIBLE Battle Group. Start helicopter Transfer of stores. In turning to flying course in heavy sea mountain of deck cargo shifts. Nasty moment. Damage guardrails. No |

The Sea King from RFA Fort Grange
—eventually it sank.

loss. Now have to run down sea and battle group have to follow! Nice to be the leader! Five hours, and all hands, to recover. Replace and relash. Still a worry. Too late to continue . . . Overnight on screen. Bouncy.

July 20   Complete Vertrep. Heavy lifts to INVINCIBLE. More mail and stores for South Georgia. Finally away. Nice farewell from INVINCIBLE who has just heard of her reprieve from sale to Australians.

22   Arrive South Georgia. Quite stunning. Snow covered and sunny. Iceberg, which was at entrance to Cumberland Bay last visit, has been blown into bay and grounded. Alongside STENA INSPECTOR to transfer stores and 2 ton anchor for WIMPEY SEAHORSE. Swell causes slight bend in garden wall! Thence into Grytviken Bay and alongside old jetty at King Edward Point. Unloaded 20 tons stores for soldiers (most of it beer and barbed wire).

23   Quiet day waiting for OLWEN to arrive with new garrison. Ship's company given tour of the whaling station. Sun with snow showers. Visit Shackletons grave and see seals and penguins of course.

24   OLWEN arrives. Alongside her to ferry new garrison stores. Soldiers have not discussed requirements and try to unload Landrover (no roads and deep snow) and more beer and food. Stop them. Back alongside Jetty. Offload. Embark outgoing Scots Guards and sail. Piper plays us out. Before ferrying them out to OLWEN carry out Combined Service gunnery shoot against iceberg! Army's anti-tank weapons remove large lumps of ice. Alongside OLWEN again offload Guards and AWAY—HOMEWARD BOUND. Hear announcement of award of South Atlantic Medal. We qualify for a medal and additional Rosette for having been where it was all happening—at the wrong time! All delighted.

Passage to Ascension. Weather beautiful in an area with greatest expectancy of foul weather in South Atlantic. Beautiful Albatross continue to follow us. Staggered and infuriated to learn that throughout the war French technicians were alleged to be arming and setting to work the Exocet missiles which killed our chums and missed us by 12 hours.

27   After 2 mirror calm days of passage north the South Atlantic has a last go at us with 40 kts on the beam, more heavy rolling and little sleep. Little sign of the Welsh Guards Major we are taking home! We have heard his sad tales about the loss of 40 of his Guards in GALAHAD with another 8 badly injured in a missile incident at Stanley. His account of the land force advance across the Falklands is riveting. It seems our Army is also the best in the world! During their 10 day advance they had only what they carried ashore. Not even a tent. Accounts of the filth left by the Argies at Stanley are unrepeatable. 16 year old lads straight from school who thought they were still in Argentina. (Our Junior Seaman Jones was not 17 until after the surrender! His first medal at 16!)

28   Weather much improved—warmth at last. Since leaving UK we have moved from spring— tropical summer—Arctic winter—summer—winter—summer. Remarkably no effect on health. Might we catch some summer at home? Deck hockey in the next day or so.

August 1   Arrived Ascension. A good sight this time. ENDURANCE just behind us and homebound after a prolonged deployment and much excitement. Advance leave party leaves for UK. Diary ends. We are due in Rosyth (via 2 days in Gibraltar), on 20 August—4 months to the day since getting the buzz in Newcastle. On our return we will have steamed 26,944 miles (once around the world) at an average speed of 16 kts. For a North Sea Fishery Protection vessel, it has been a wonderful experience.

Both HMS Leeds Castle and her sister HMS Dumbarton Castle ferried endless amounts of stores and personnel around the fleet. A visitor is pictured being lowered to HMS Dumbarton Castle's flight deck. The Sea King obviously couldn't land because of the mass of stores temporarily stowed on the flight deck.

## HMS GLASGOW

The main concentration of Argentinian troops and support was at Port Stanley and HMS GLASGOW was sent inshore to carry out naval gunfire support on selected targets in the area, she fired over 180 rounds of 4.5″ ammunition on her first stint on the gunline.

Two days later HMS GLASGOW went inshore again—whilst engaging targets ashore, three waves of four aircraft attacked GLASGOW at low level coming from over the land. Of the first wave an accompanying frigate shot down 2 aircraft with Sea Wolf missiles—a third cartwheeled into the sea. The third wave turned back without pressing home the attack! However, the middle wave kept coming—despite the upperdeck action crew firing every conceivable small weapon at them. One of these aircraft dropped a bomb which entered the after engine room, passed over the main machinery and flew out of the other side. The immediate problem after the raid was stopping the sea pouring into the ship.

Damage control parties swung into action. Pumps were started and mattresses pushed into the three foot hole. As time progressed and the extent of the damage became clearer more substantial wooden shoring was erected to slow the flood of water; stopping it completely would have to wait. HMS GLASGOW sailed to the edge of the TEZ. There, in heavy seas, which made welding difficult, she patched up her holes and returned to her air defence station within three days. HMS INVINCIBLE provided gear and hands to help.

One of the biggest problems arose because the hole was on the waterline. Welding is straight forward in air or underwater but impossible in a mixture of the two. To overcome this the ship was heeled over by shifting fuel and driving the ship round and round in circles. Despite continuing leaks, damaged equipment and loss of remote control to the main engines, HMS GLASGOW returned to her station to provide air defence for the carriers and support ships, until after the landing, and the arrival of another air defence ship from the UK. She was then ordered to return to UK for repairs.

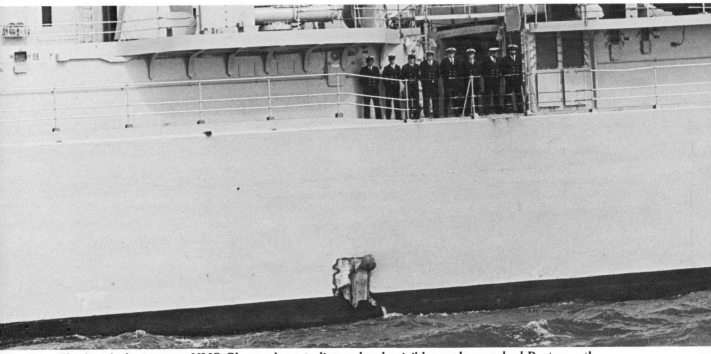

The bomb damage on HMS Glasgow's waterline—clearly visible as she reached Portsmouth.

## HMS CARDIFF

Tidying up HMS Cardiff's fo'c's'le after a naval gunfire support session during which she fired 277 rounds.

## STENA SEASPREAD—FANTASTIC SHIP

The Seaspread Class of four vessels are designed as diving and support vessels to the oil industry, with firefighting and evacuation facilities. Built to the highest Ice Class she has stabilisation tanks capable of reducing roll by up to 75%. Position keeping is by a Kongsberg Dynamic Positioning computer-operated system which controls the vessels five propellers. This is designed to hold the vessel in position at all attitudes to the wind-up to wind force 9. A four point anchoring system is fitted, capable of anchoring the vessel in 1500 ft. of water. The ship is built to passenger ship safety standards. The vessel has diesel electric propulsion. The engine room is designed to run unmanned at night whilst on passage. As a supply vessel, the ship can carry:- 2100 tons oil, 550 tons Drill Water, 300 tons Fresh Water, 312 cu.m. Cement and up to about 2,000 tons of deck cargo. The diving bell has an operating depth of 300 m and an observation depth of 450 metres. There is a 12 man saturation system capable of simultaneous operation at 2 different depths. Accommodation is to a high standard. There is a 5-bedded hospital and treatment room, and a well equipped totally stainless steel galley.

## — FANTASTIC JOB

The sight of MSV STENA SEASPREAD (Captain M. Williams M.N.) steaming backwards, forwards and sideways around the ocean and anchorages became a familiar sight in the South Atlantic. An extremely powerful vessel, capable of 4½ knots sideways, she caused a great deal of interest to all. Fitted with good workshop facilities and cranes up to 100 tons, the vessel was ideally suited to be adapted to a Heavy Repair Ship for the Falklands Campaign. The decision to do so was taken on the Thursday before Easter, and she sailed for the South Atlantic 8 days later.

The embarked Naval Party, commanded by Captain Paul Badcock Royal Navy, consisted of a large team of skilled engineering ratings. Also in the Naval Party, to keep the technocrats supplied with food, clothing, spare parts and materials, was a Supply and Secretariat team; and to keep them healthy and repair the inevitable cuts and bruises that engineering brings, a Medical Officer and Leading Medical Assistant. General oganisation, seamanship and liaison between the Royal Navy and Merchant Navy in matters such as operations, communications and navigation was looked after by the First Lieutenants' team of seamen and communicators.

STENA SEASPREAD was hurriedly recalled from the Thistle oil field, first to Peterhead and then into Portsmouth Dockyard: so rapid was this recall there were still divers in the saturation chambers on her arrival at Portsmouth on Easter Monday. In a period of 4 days the ship underwent a miraculous transformation to her new role. New workshops, stores and messdecks were built, and an extensive communication fit was installed. The overwhelming impression was of lorries queuing for the cranes to hoist their loads onto the ship—almost faster than they could be struck down. She sailed at just before midnight on April 16.

A few days were spent in the sun at Ascension loading yet more stores and embarking the balance of the Naval Party. It was at Ascension that our first "customers" were dealt with, including HMS ARDENT and HMS ANTELOPE.

Ascension was soon left astern as the ship headed for South Georgia, pausing en route only to receive yet more stores, airdropped by Hercules aircraft into the sea, to be recovered by Gemini dinghies. This period was also used to work up effective damage control, firefighting and first aid teams, manned by both RN and MN personnel.

The ungainly but essential repair ship, Stena Seaspread.

Ships damaged off the Falklands needed urgent repairs. More steel was needed. A working party from HMS Endurance soon got to work "liberating" steel from the whaling station at South Georgia (the same one that the Argentinian scrapmen landed to demolish earlier in the spring). The steel was transferred to the Cable Ship Iris for delivery to the Repair Ship "Stena Seaspread". It was then used to patch up a variety of ships before they set off on their long haul northwards and home . . .

## STENA SEASPREAD

South Georgia was initially chosen as the repair base for the Task Force. On arrival there teams were set to work in the old whaling stations at Leith and Stromness, which had been abandoned some 20 years ago. At Stromness, which had been the repair yard for the whale catchers, there was a wealth of ship repairing material and equipment. The generating station was set to work, the canteen cleared and galley range restored to working order and fresh water supplies surveyed.

However, as the crisis developed it became apparent the repair team would need to be closer to the Battle Group, resulting in a move to the edge of the Total Exclusion Zone known as the "TARA" (Tug and Repair Area), and later another area known as the "TRALA" (Towing, Repair and Logistic Area). It was here that the work really started, repairing battle damaged ships in uncomfortable and hazardous conditions. Despite the difficulties and hardships much excellent work was achieved. Additionally, teams were despatched to ships in "Bomb Alley". They carried out "on site" repairs and maintenance while the battle raged about them. The aim was to return a ship as an effective fighting unit as quickly as possible. If the damage was too severe for that, repairs were made to allow the ship to complete the 8,000 mile journey back to UK safely. It would be impossible to detail all the work that was done. The list of ships repaired speaks for itself—11 "cases" of battle damage and over 30 ships requiring other maintenance. Some incidents stood out, such as that of HMS PLYMOUTH. Having spent 4 days repairing damage caused by 3 bombs, all of which fortunately failed to explode (though one set off a depth charge on deck), PLYMOUTH sailed back for the battle area capable of 85% power and with all weapons except her mortar serviceable. Her gesture of appreciation in lining her ship's side and cheering the repair teams was much appreciated. Another seriously damaged ship was HMS GLAMORGAN following an Exocet hit near her hangar. Much effort went into re-establishing the integrity of the hull, and into restoring 70% of the main galley which had been devastated by the explosion of the missile. Whilst their own galley was being renovated, HMS GLAMORGAN's ships company was fed from SEASPREAD. It was no mean feat to feed 700 men from a galley designed to feed 70!

A typical example of the improvisation necessary to provide a full repair service despite logistic difficulties was provided during the repair of one of GLAMORGAN's galley machines. A weld was required in a piece of stainless steel; although the welding equipment was suitable no stainless steel welding rods were carried. The problem was overcome by using a pair of stainless steel dessert spoons to provide the welding filler!

When the flow of battle-damaged ships finally, and thankfully, ceased, it was replaced by all the other ships with defects requiring rectification. By this time it was possible to move into the calmer, and by now peaceful, anchorage of San Carlos Water. The new role was tackled with equal enthusiasm, resulting in many satisfied customers. During this period two Royal Navy "firsts" were achieved: The first controllable pitch propeller blade change carried out afloat (HMS AVENGER), and the first Gas Turbine Change Unit exchange for a destroyer or frigate at anchor (HMS SOUTHAMPTON). Both of these jobs went as planned and well within the allocated time schedules. In the case of the engine change, this was completed in less than 48 hours, and carried out in cold, snowy weather. Both "firsts" earned a commendation from C in C Fleet at Northwood.

In addition to the RN and RFA ships, assistance was also rendered to a number of merchant ships involved in the campaign. Also, work was done on 4 ships that had been captured from, or abandoned by, the Argentine forces.

At the request of the senior officer of the 4th Frigate Squadron the men on board STENA SEASPREAD manufactured the 30 foot memorial erected overlooking San Carlos Water. It is visible from the two points where the two ships of the Squadron were lost—ARDENT and ANTELOPE.

## ATLANTIC CONVEYOR

ATLANTIC CONVEYOR was hit by at least one, possibly two, Exocet missiles just before dusk on May 25 as she closed on the British beachhead at San Carlos Water . It quickly became obvious that the 14,950 ton container ship would have to be abandoned, and the evacuation was completed in about 15 minutes. She was eventually gutted by fire.

Shortly before the red alert warning of imminent attack flashed to ATLANTIC CONVEYOR's bridge, a Royal Navy team had launched a Wessex helicopter from the bow. These men were cut off from the rest of the ship by the heat and smoke, but were picked off the deck by a Wessex and a Sea King.

Three of the four Chinook heavy lift helicopters were destroyed (the fourth was away at the time) as were six Wessex helicopters and a large quantity of spares for these helicopters and Harriers. The Harrier aircraft she had been transporting had been flown off earlier.

Twelve men died in the attack, including the ship's master, Capt. Ian North. Three of those lost were Royal Navy personnel, and three were from the RFA, with six from Cunard.

With cluster bombs exploding in her holds, an escort frigate closed bravely on the crippled and burning ship to play water on her steaming sides. Lines were thrown to the liferafts in the water, and the last survivors were picked up about two and a half hours after leaving the CONVEYOR.

Still burning 24 hours after the missile struck.

The end of a fine ship . . .

# THE AIR WAR

In any war fought 8,000 miles from the home base air power will these days play a significant role—both in maintaining and supporting the lines of supply and communication and, of course, in the actual fighting.

In the Falklands campaign the air war story divides easily into those two categories with the work of the RAF dominating the former and the latter shared by all the services—Helicopters from the Fleet Air Arm, RAF, Army Air Corps and Royal Marines worked together in the amphibious area while RN Sea Harries and RAF Harriers provided air cover and highly mobile firepower to hit the enemy on the battlefield—and well behind the lines.

Helicopters proved themselves the workhorses of the force—carrying men, stores, flying support missions armed with guns, rockets and missiles, conducting anti-submarine, anti-surface ship and chaff missions, recce patrols—the list seems never ending.

Backing them up was the air defence and ground attack muscle of the RN Sea Harriers and the RAF Harriers. The Fleet sailed with less than 30 fixed wing aircraft. They faced an airforce with 250 operational combat aircraft. Those odds were greater than the "Few" faced during the Battle of Britain.

Combat air patrols were the daily grind of the Sea Harriers—they flew more than 2,000 and became the bogey of the Argentine pilots. Lt Cdr Nigel "Sharky" Ward, Commanding Officer of 809 Squadron, said the Argentines never engaged in air combat. As soon as they saw the Sea Harriers they dropped their bombs and returned to base. This was not a sign of cowardice—but their Mirages and Skyhawks were not equipped with air to air missiles nor did they have fuel to dog fight and fly home from their targets. The opposite was true, the Argentine pilots exhibited great skill and tremendous bravery in pressing home their attacks on shipping in San Carlos Water. Overall the Argentines lost six out of every ten aircraft they launched on raids. It must have needed great courage for a returning pilot to get airborne again heading for the Falklands a few days later.

The Navy committed 171 aircraft, fixed wing and rotary, to the operation. These were deployed in 14 Squadrons—including four new ones which were commissioned in record time. Overall they achieved more than 90% availability of aircraft. The Navy's Sea Harriers achieved 27 kills of enemy aircraft. Many more were shot down by anti-aircraft fire: Rapiers 13 credited kills; Seacat 6 credited kills; Sea Wolf 5 credited kills; Sea Dart 8 credited kills; 4.5" gun 1 credited kill; Bofors/small arms/hand held missiles 3 credited kills; Own goal 4; Destroyed on ground 26.

RAF Harriers, mostly from No. 1 Squadron joined the Task Force to add to the efforts of the hard pressed Sea Harriers. Some arrived onboard ATLANTIC CONVEYOR and luckily were flown off before she was hit by Exocet—although many valuable spares on board were lost. Others arrived in CONTENDER BEZANT, while four aircraft flew all the way to HMS Hermes from UK with only a stop at Ascension. They were refuelled in the air from Victor tankers for this record breaking 8,000 mile flight, 18 hours straight into the combat zone.


Inter-service rivalries were forgotten in the South Atlantic, everyone was in the same team. Here an RAF GR3 Harrier is pictured with an RN Sea Harrier, flying over HMS Broadsword. RAF Harrier is optimised for ground attack but has a limited air defence capability, while the Sea Harriers Blue Fox radar makes it a very effective interceptor. Both types are highly manoeuvrable thanks to their ability to vector their engine thrust, and so can more than hold their own in dog fights.

The RAF Harriers, best suited as ground attack aircraft, were fitted with Sidewinder air to air missiles and given a secondary air defence role. These Harriers flew 150 sorties against positions defended by anti-aircraft guns and missiles, with the loss of just three aircraft.

A forward operating base was set up at Port San Carlos and an aluminium runway landing pad, taxi ways and refuelling facilities were installed. A couple of aircraft normally remained there on instant readiness to scramble to fight off Argentine raids approaching from the west.

The helicopters flew round the clock in all weathers. At sea there were constant anti-submarine patrols and extensive cross decking operations, over land there was intensive ferrying of stores and men. In particular the solitary heavy lift Chinook—the others were sunk with ATLANTIC CONVEYOR—was a familiar sight and sound to all the troops. Known as Bravo November from her identification code she was regarded with affection by everyone despite her propensity to demolish "friendly" tents with her rotors powerful downwash!

This Chinook with a handful of ground and air crew under the command of Squadron Leader Dick Langworthy lost all their spares, tools, ground support equipment, tents and communications equipment in ATLANTIC CONVEYOR. Somehow, they kept Bravo November in the air, and from 27 May until 23 June, when reinforcements arrived, she flew 1530 troops, 600 tons of equipment and 650 PoW's. In one sortie alone she flew 81 troops of 5 Brigade forward to Fitzroy—then in an unsecured area. Normally Chinooks carry 30 men!

The eighty Sea Kings and Wessex helicopters provided tactical mobility and a logistic lifeline to the units fighting over terrain where otherwise only mules could have coped. HMS ENDURANCE's Wasp with HMS GLAMORGAN's Wessex successfully attacked the Argentine submarine SANTA FE and Lynx helicopters fired the first Sea Skua missiles operationally.

The medical evacuaction chain would not have even existed without the ubiquitous helicopters. Even so there were never enough "choppers", and the sinking of ATLANTIC CONVEYOR with three Chinooks and 6 Wessex onboard was a severe loss.

One result of this dire shortage of helicopters was that many soldiers—principally from 45 Commando and 3 Para weren't able to fly forward to the battle area but had to march—in some cases 80 miles.

While helicopters provided the initial links in the chain back to UK, RAF VC10s in the aero-medical role provided the final link home. Wounded, once their condition was stabilised in the Hospital Ship SS UGANDA, were taken by ambulance ship to Montivideo, from there they were air-lifted 7,000 miles to UK in VC10s distinctively marked with Red Crosses.

A Victor tanker refuelling a Nimrod.

Meanwhile the RAF were ferrying mail and essential stores to Ascension and carrying them on from there in Hercules to be parachuted into the sea near the Task Force. A small number of Hercules were given long range tanks and an air to air refuelling capability—designed, tested and operationally proved in just a few weeks. Under normal circumstances it would have taken two years or more.

At the time of the surrender plans were well advanced for a scheme whereby Hercules would "snatch" small loads of mail and essential cargo from either ships at sea or the troops on land. This scheme was subsequently used when Stanley airfield was closed for repairs and extending.

These Hercules were converted because the Task Force steamed south beyond the aircraft's normal range. Eventually the Task Force was so far away from the Hercules forward operating base at Ascension that new endurance records were being set—almost daily. One remarkable record must be that of Flt Lt Terry Locke who flew his Hercules on an airdrop mission to East Falklands for 28 hours 3 minutes. The air transport effort was staggering, more than 17,000 hours were flown, 13,000 of them by the faithful Hercules.

Nimrod maritime patrol aircraft were also fitted to refuel in the air and they maintained continuous patrols and were cleared to carry Sidewinder air to air missiles and Harpoon air to surface missiles. Vulcan bombers attacked Port Stanley airfield and they too had to refuel in the air. This meant a heavy work load on the Victor tankers, to help out four Hercules were converted to airborne tankers—again in record time.

A Hercules tanker refuelling a Hercules transport during the long flight from Ascension to Port Stanley.

This conversion helped with mid-air refuelling of the Hercules. Problems had been discovered in filling up a Hercules from a Victor tanker. The Victors operating speed was slightly higher than the cruising speed of a Hercules. A procedure was developed for the Hercules to connect its refuelling probe into the "basket" reeled out astern of the Victor and then for both aircraft to go into shallow dive which gave the Hercules the extra speed required. Very skilled airmanship! Another problem was the Hercules with its large control surface area suffered in the considerable turbulence created by the Victor's powerful engines. The Victor normally refuels much smaller fighter aircraft. These speed and turbulence problems were eased with the introduction of the new Hercules tanker aircraft. The need for tankers was so acute the Victors carried out 600 sorties and six Vulcan bombers were also converted for the urgent fuelling requirement.

The Vulcan bomber force rundown was half complete when the conflict started. Despite many years assigned to low level nuclear operations in the NATO area, the Vulcan with its long range and ability to carry a heavy bomb load clearly had a new role to play.

Conventional bombing and air to air refuelling had not been used or practised for 10 years but within three weeks crews had been trained and aircraft deployed to Ascension. The Vulcan raids on Port Stanley are the longest range bombing missions in the history of air warfare. Three attacks were made against the runway and two against early warning radar positions. They were made at night to take advantage of the aircrafts blind bombing capability and from 10,000 feet to minimise risk from the powerful air defences. Each mission lasted 15-16 hours.

These attacks, whilst they didn't totally destroy the runway (it is extremely difficult using conventional bombs) did prevent high performance Mirages, Skyhawks and Super Etendard aircraft from operating from it. They were thus forced to operate at extreme range from airfields on the mainland.

As all these missions were mounted from Ascension and as mounds of stores built up there it became obvious this island was a high value asset and an attractive target. Air defence was arranged initially using Harriers and later Phantom Interceptors. Aircraft movements from the island increased from 40 per month before the conflict to peak at 400-per-day during it! Indeed, being the nearest airfield to the operational area and the success of providing support over such large distances is one of the greatest achievements of the campaign.

A Hercules being refuelled from a Vulcan bomber—converted to a tanker during the conflict.

A Royal Navy Sea Harrier aircraft is pictured here on the flight deck of HMS Fearless in San Carlos Water. The temporary airstrip for Harriers rapidly constructed at Port San Carlos ran out of fuel a few days before the surrender and the two Harriers normally on standby there against Argentine air attacks were temporarily redeployed to HMS Fearless and HMS Intrepid, both anchored in the loch nearby. Normally these ships only operate helicopters, but such is their versatility they acted as Harrier carriers for an afternoon. In fact both aircraft were scrambled from their decks to intercept an incoming air raid.

An RAF Hercules lands at the desolate Port Stanley airfield after a 13 hour flight from Ascension. The Pucara aircraft in the foreground were wrecked by Argentine prisoners of war when they were all collected together in large numbers at the airfield after the surrender.

Wessex and Sea King helicopters carried their "self defence" with them. The gunner pictured here is PO Aircrewman Arthur Ball of 845 Squadron. He fired the missile which hit Stanley Police Station—when being used by the Argentinians.

A Chinook heavy lift helicopter about to lift an underslung load from HMS Intrepid's flight deck at Ascension.

A crucial underslung load, ammunition from Teal Inlet for the gunners on Mount Kent—every load was desperately needed at the front . . .

Not exactly Heathrow . . . refuelling a Scout of the Commando Brigade Air Squadron at the Forward Air Base at Teal Inlet.

# VICTORY AT LAST . . .

The end came suddenly. Argentine soldiers retreated in droves, white flags were seen over Stanley. There were negotiations for a surrender and the British troops took over.

They found chaos and filth everywhere — the number of surrendering soldiers was greater than the British staff believed the Argentinians had sent to the Islands. The Argentines didn't even have accurate numbers or records of their own forces.

By and large the Argentines were well equipped and there was plenty of food, but they didn't seem to have a logistics organisation which could cope with getting supplies out from Stanley. There were reports of men starving in isolated observation posts, others being reduced to stealing dogs' bones and chicken feed — while nearby units had plenty of rations.

The bulk of the Argentine forces were in Stanley. They were herded off to the airport — which is on a peninsula — so that they could easily be controlled. On the way they passed through a check point where they were disarmed. The pile of discarded weapons became a small mountain. In the town there were similar, but smaller, weapons dumps and live ammunition littered the streets.

At the airfield there was little or no shelter from the bone-chilling 35 knot wind direct from the Antarctic. The Argentines had destroyed all the tents earmarked for Prisoners when they sank the ATLANTIC CONVEYOR. The British Command had fears there would be a disaster in which many more Argentine troops would die than were killed in action. The answer was for the Argentine government to give safe conduct to vessels carrying the prisoners home. After several days of diplomatic pressure this clearance was obtained and swiftly the demoralised PoW's sailed to ports in Southern Argentina.

Meanwhile gangs of prisoners under guard cleaned up the town which they had left in an appallingly filthy state. Everywhere were weapons, live ammunition, military equipment, field guns, armoured cars, trucks and mines. The Argentine forces had scattered mines from helicopters but had not kept maps of their locations — a vicious legacy for the future. But a small number of Argentine sappers volunteered to stay behind and help clear these death traps from the countryside.

Major General Jeremy Moore proudly holds the surrender document.

The Surrender Document. The Argentine Commander deleted and initialed the word 'unconditionally' on the second line.

Major General Jeremy Moore, Commander Land Forces Falkland Islands, meets a young islander who really isn't aware the Argentinians have surrendered or even who they were . . .

Royal Marines of J Company, 42 Commando (originally Naval Party 8901) who defended the Islands during the Argentine invasion. They soon returned to hoist the Union Flag (with the Falklands emblem) at Government House, Stanley.

Argentine PoW's wait in the filthy streets of Stanley to be called forward for embarkation and the voyage home.

Argentine PoW's clean up Stanley after the surrender. They are guarded by Royal Marines of 45 Commando.

Homeward bound, Argentine prisoners sleep on the deck in Canberra—at least it was warm and dry.
Lice ridden Argentine helmets ditched in the sea from Canberra as she steams to Argentina full of PoW's being repatriated.

The pile of discarded weapons beside the road to Stanley airfield.

A lethal lorry load . . . Exocet missiles in their containers on the back of a trailer. HMS Glamorgan was hit by one of these land based missiles.

Panhard armoured cars in Port Stanley, so new that even the insides of their engine compartments were spotless.

The captured Argentine oil rig support vessel Yehuin. She was soon set to work in Stanley harbour ferrying prisoners and stores.

When the war was over one of the major problems was locating and clearing mines. The Argentines had scattered mines from helicopters and hadn't kept proper maps of their locations. Many of these mines were small and made of a plastic substance and thus were extremely difficult to detect. Here sappers of 59 Independent Commando Squadron Royal Engineers are pictured clearing a minefield at Stanley Airport.

An old seaplane hangar is used as temporary shelter for Royal Marine Commandos. The doors tell their own story . . .

The Paras arrive in Stanley.

British troops remained vigilant even after surrender.

105

Local girls pause for a chat with men of 42 Commando soon after liberation. Stanley police station is behind.

A famous visitor to Stanley soon after the surrender! HRH Prince Andrew flew in by Sea King to take a look for himself.

# TIME TO GO HOME

Snowballs on the Equator! They were made in the Falklands and kept in HMS Ambuscade's deep freeze for this memorable "crossing the line" on the way home.

A sailor's view of a typical homecoming. Days never to be forgotten . . .

# AT PLYMOUTH

The Red Arrows say Welcome Home to "their" ship—HMS Arrow.

Hospital Ship Uganda.

# AT SOUTHAMPTON

# AT PORTSMOUTH

BATTERED—BUT BACK, HMS Hermes receives a fantastic welcome.

HMS Endurance too.

# AT CHATHAM

# AT ROSYTH

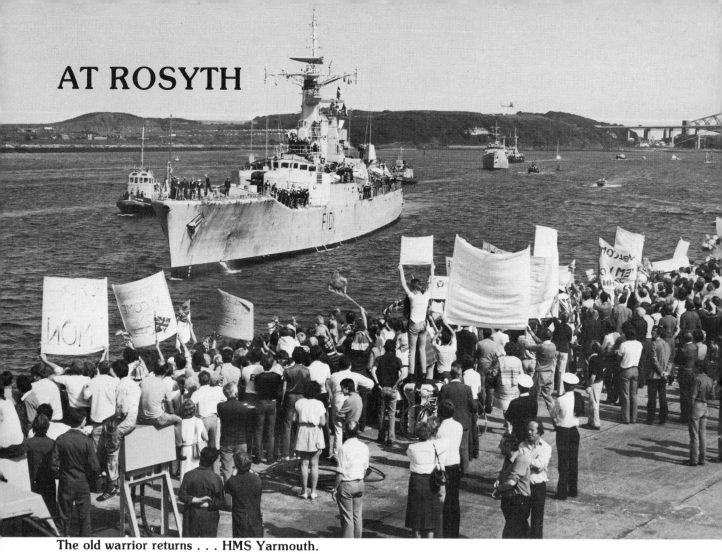

The old warrior returns . . . HMS Yarmouth.

Some crowd . . . HMS Plymouth, gets the VIP treatment.

# PARTICIPATING FORCES

## ROYAL NAVY

**Aircraft Carriers**
HMS INVINCIBLE
HMS HERMES

**Assault Ships**
HMS FEARLESS
HMS INTREPID

**Destroyers**
HMS ANTRIM
HMS GLAMORGAN
HMS COVENTRY
HMS CARDIFF
HMS GLASGOW
HMS SHEFFIELD
HMS EXETER
HMS BRISTOL

**Ice Patrol Ship**
HMS ENDURANCE

**Survey Vessels**
HMS HECLA
HMS HYDRA
HMS HERALD
HMS HECATE

**MCMV**
HMS BRECON
HMS LEDBURY

**Frigates**
HMS ARDENT
HMS ANTELOPE
HMS ACTIVE
HMS ALACRITY
HMS AMBUSCADE
HMS ARROW
HMS AVENGER
HMS YARMOUTH
HMS PLYMOUTH
HMS BRILLIANT
HMS BROADSWORD
HMS ARGONAUT
HMS ANDROMEDA
HMS MINERVA
HMS PENELOPE

**Submarines**
HMS COURAGEOUS
HMS CONQUEROR
HMS SPLENDID
HMS SPARTAN
HMS VALIANT
HMS ONYX

**Despatch Vessels**
HMS LEEDS CASTLE
HMS DUMBARTON
    CASTLE

## ARMY

**Royal Armoured Corps**
Royal Horse Guards

**Royal Artillery**
12 Air Defence Regiment
29 Commando Regiment
21 Air Defence Battery, 27 Field Regiment
  4 Field Regiment
43 Battery, 32 Guided Weapons Regiment

**Royal Engineers**
36 Engineer Regiment
11 Field Squadron (Harrier Support)
59 Independent Commando Squadron
49 Explosive Ordnance Disposal Squadron
50 Field Squadron

**Royal Signals**
5 Infantry Brigade HQ and Signals Squadron
Elements of 30 Signal Regiment
602 Signals Troop
Elements of 14 Signal Regiment

**Infantry**
2nd Battalion, Scots Guards
1st Battalion, Welsh Guards
1/7th Gurkha Rifles
2nd Battalion, Parachute Regiment
3rd Battalion, Parachute Regiment
Special Air Service

**Army Air**
656 Squadron, Army Air Corps

**Royal Corps of Transport**
Port Squadron, 17 Port Regiment
47 Air Despatch Squadron

**Royal Army Medical Corps**
2 Field Hospital
16 Field Ambulance

**Royal Army Ordnance Corps**
9 Ordnance Battalion
81 Ordnance Company
91 Ordnance Company
Elements 42 Explosive Ordnance Company

**Royal Electrical and Mechanical Engineers**
10 Field Workshops

**Royal Military Police**
160 Provost Company

**Royal Army Pay Corps**
Field Cash Office

**Intelligence Corps**
172 Intelligence and Security Section

**Royal Marines**
40 Commando
42 Commando
45 Commando
Commando Logistic Regiment
3 Commando Brigade HQ and
    Signals Squadron
3 Commando Brigade Air Squadron
3 Commando Brigade Air Defence Troop
1 Raiding Squadron
Mountain and Arctic Warfare Cadre
Commando Forces Band
Special Boat Section

## RAF

| | |
|---|---|
| **VULCANS** from | 44, 50, & 101 Squadrons |
| **NIMRODS** from | 42, 120, 201, & 206 Squadrons |
| **HERCULES** from | 24, 30, 47, & 70 Squadrons |
| **VC10s** from | 10 Squadron |
| **VICTORS** from | 55, 57 Squadrons |
| **HARRIERS** from | 1 Squadron |
| **CHINOOKS** from | 18 Squadron |
| **SEA KING HELICOPTERS** from | 202 Squadron |

**RAF Regiment**
Elements of No. 3 Wing
15 Squadron
63 (Rapier) Squadron

## RFAs

FORT AUSTIN
FORT GRANGE
SIR GALAHAD
SIR LANCELOT
SIR GERAINT
SIR TRISTRAM
SIR PERCIVALE
SIR BEDIVERE
STROMNESS
TIDESPRING
TIDEPOOL
REGENT
RESOURCE
ENGADINE
OLNA
OLMEDA
BAYLEAF
APPLELEAF
PEARLEAF
PLUMLEAF
BRAMBLELEAF
BLUE ROVER

## RMAS

TYPHOON
GOOSANDER

### Merchant Navy

| | |
|---|---|
| AVELONA STAR | GEEST PORT |
| ASTRONOMER | G.A. WALKER |
| ANCO CHARGER | IRIS |
| ALVEGA | IRISHMAN |
| ATLANTIC CONVEYOR | JUNELLA |
| ATLANTIC CAUSEWAY | LYCAON |
| BRITISH AVON | LAERTES |
| BRITISH DART | MYRMIDON |
| BRITISH ESK | NORTHELLA |
| BRITISH TAMAR | NORDIC FERRY |
| BRITISH TAY | NORLAND |
| BRITISH TEST | PICT |
| BRITISH TRENT | QUEEN ELIZABETH 2 |
| BRITISH WYE | RANGATIRA |
| BALDER LONDON | SALVAGEMAN |
| BALTIC FERRY | SAXONIA |
| BRITISH ENTERPRISE III | STENA INSPECTOR |
| CEDAR BANK | STENA SEASPREAD |
| CORDELLA | STRATHEWE |
| CANBERRA | SCOTTISH EAGLE |
| CONTENDER BEZANT | ST. HELENA |
| ELK | TOR CALEDONIA |
| EBURNA | UGANDA |
| EUROPIC FERRY | WIMPEY SEAHORSE |
| FARNELLA | YORKSHIREMAN |
| FORT TORONTO | |

# A SOUTH ATLANTIC DIARY — (continued)

**May 12**
Argentine Skyhawks attack warships bombarding Port Stanley targets. Four Skyhawks reported destroyed, two with Sea Wolf missiles. Bomb passes through HMS Glasgow without exploding. Sea King ditches. Crew rescued.

**May 14**
Sir Anthony Parsons, Britain's envoy at the United Nations, and Sir Nicholas Henderson, Britain's Ambassador to the United States, fly home from U.N. peace negotiations for urgent talks with Mrs. Thatcher.

**May 14/15**
Pebble Island airfield, radar installation and ammunition dump destroyed by Royal Marines ground force, SAS and naval bombardment. Marines sustain two minor casualties, 11 aircraft destroyed on ground. Sea Harriers bomb Falklands targets.

**May 16**
Bombardment of military installations in the Falklands by British warships continues. Two Argentine supply vessels damaged by Sea Harriers in the Falkland Sound. A third Argentine merchant ship, the Rio Carcarana, is bombed and strafed in Port King Bay and a supply vessel moored close to Fox Bay settlement is strafed.

**May 17**
Sea King ditches after instrument failure. Crew rescued. Argentine Air Force commander, Brigadier Basilico Lami Dozo, warns that British task force will receive massive attack if it sails within range of Argentinian weapons.

**May 18**
Hopes fade for a successful outcome to United Nations peace negotiations.

**May 19**
British troop-carrying helicopter ditches between ships in the task force and 21 soldiers are killed. Substantial bombardment of military targets south of Port Stanley and in East Falkland by British warships and Sea Harriers.

**May 20**
Royal Navy Sea King helicopter crashes in mysterious circumstances on a beach near Punta Arenas in Chile. Crew of three burn their machine and go into hiding.
First RAF Harrier attack on Port Stanley. They also bomb fuel dump in Fox Bay.

**May 21**
Britain lands several thousand troops near Port San Carlos, 50 miles west of Port Stanley. During fierce Argentine air attack on British invasion force in Falkland Sound, HMS Ardent, is sunk with loss of 22 men. Four other warships are damaged. British flag is raised again in Falklands as troops establish bridgehead. 20 Argentine aircraft destroyed.

**May 23**
HMS Antelope, badly damaged and set on fire during air attack in Falkland Sound—one man killed and five injured. Eight Argentine planes are destroyed and one British Sea Harrier lost. One Argentine helicopter shot down in Falkland Sound and another crashes on fire. Britain consolidates her bridgehead with 5,000 troops reported dug in with anti-aircraft weapons.

**May 24**
HMS Antelope sinks. Nine Argentine aircraft shot down. LSLs Sir Galahad and Sir Lancelot damaged in air attack in San Carlos Water.

**May 25**
Britain loses destroyer HMS Coventry (24 men killed) and the Cunard container ship, Atlantic Conveyor (nine dead) during intensive air attacks as Argentina celebrates her Independence Day. 5 Argentine aircraft splashed.

**May 27**
263 survivors from HMS Sheffield fly home to be greeted by joyous families. RAF Harriers attack Stanley airport and Goose Green—one shot down, pilot ejected behind enemy lines, later recovered. One Argentine Skyhawk splashed, one damaged.

**May 28**
Port Darwin settlement and Goose Green airstrip captured by British/paratroopers after fierce fighting. Lt-Col H. Jones, commander of the 2nd Bn. The Parachute Regiment, among 17 British troops killed. About 250 Argentine soldiers believed killed and 1,400 taken prisoner.

**May 30**
The men who died at Port Darwin and Goose Green are buried together in a mass grave on a hillside above the anchorage at San Carlos Water. Royal Marines advancing towards Port Stanley capture Douglas Settlement and Teal Inlet.

**May 31**
Task force troops reach Mount Kent, 12 miles west of Port Stanley. Argentine aircraft attack British ships with bombs and missiles but are beaten off without damage or casualties. Two Skyhawk aircraft shot down. Atlantic Conveyor, devastated by Exocet missile on May 25, sinks. Vulcan and Harrier attacks in East Falkland.

**June 1**
British troops take Mount Kent, 12 miles from Port Stanley. Two RAF Harriers fly direct from Ascension to HMS Hermes.

**June 2**
With British forces occupying high ground eight miles from Port Stanley, Argentinian troops are under attack by land, sea and air. Mrs. Thatcher offers Argentina last chance to withdraw before further loss of life. Two task force Harriers ditch after raids on Port Stanley—pilots are rescued. Three Argentine prisoners killed in explosion of ammunition at Goose Green. Hercules aircraft clock up 3 million miles flying.

**June 6**
Fitzroy and Bluff Cove are taken.

**June 8**
Britain suffers its heaviest casualties on the grimmest day of the war. 43 soldiers and seven seamen die when the landing ships Sir Galahad and Sir Tristram are bombed and strafed at Fitzroy. Six men die when a landing craft from HMS Fearless is destroyed by aircraft in Choiseul Sound. Five men are injured when the frigate, HMS Plymouth, is attacked in Falkland Sound. Eleven Argentine aircraft are shot down. Two further RAF Harriers fly direct to HMS Hermes from Ascension.

**June 11**
The QE2, carrying 700 survivors of sunken warships HMS Coventry, HMS Ardent, and HMS Antelope, arrives back in Southampton to tumultuous welcome from families and friends. British troops advance to within ten miles of Port Stanley.

**June 12**
HMS Glamorgan hit by shore-based Exocet missile, 13 killed, 14 wounded. Argentine defences in hills overlooking Port Stanley are overrun by British forces who take 400 prisoners.

**June 13**
British troops rout Argentinians in Tumbledown Mountain, Mount William and Wireless Ridge, and storm on to the outskirts of Port Stanley. Neutral zone set up in capital for 600 civilians.

**June 14**
Argentine forces surrender. Troops enter Stanley.

# HONOURS AND AWARDS
## ARMY DEPARTMENT

Lt. Col. 'H' Jones V.C.

Sgt. Ian McKay V.C.

## VICTORIA CROSS

Lieutenant Colonel Herbert Jones O.B.E., The Parachute Regiment.

On 28th May 1982 Lieutenant Colonel JONES was commanding 2nd Battalion The Parachute Regiment on operations on the Falkland Islands. The Battalion was ordered to attack enemy positions in and around the settlements of Darwin and Goose Green.

During the attack against an enemy who was well dug in with mutually supporting positions sited in depth, the Battalion was held up just South of Darwin by a particularly well-prepared and resilient enemy position of at least eleven trenches on an important ridge. A number of casualties were received. In order to read the battle fully and to ensure that the momentum of his attack was not lost, Colonel Jones took forward his reconnaissance party to the foot of a re-entrant which a section of his Battalion had just secured. Despite persistent, heavy and accurate fire the reconnaissance party gained the top of the re-entrant, at approximately the same height as the enemy positions. From here Colonel Jones encouraged the direction of his Battalion mortar fire, in an effort to neutralise the enemy positions. However, these had been well prepared and continued to pour effective fire onto the Battalion advance, which, by now held up for over an hour and under increasingly heavy artillery fire, was in danger of faltering.

In his effort to gain a good viewpoint, Colonel Jones was now at the very front of his Battalion. It was clear to him that desperate measures were needed in order to overcome the enemy position and rekindle the attack, and that unless these measures were taken promptly the Battalion would sustain increasing casualties and the attack perhaps even fail. It was time for personal leadership and action. Colonel Jones immediately seized a sub-machine gun, and, calling on those around him and with total disregard for his own safety, charged the nearest enemy position. This action exposed him to fire from a number of trenches. As he charged up a short slope at the enemy position he was seen to fall and roll backward downhill. He immediately picked himself up, and again charged the enemy trench, firing his sub-machine gun and seemingly oblivious to the intense fire directed at him. He was hit by fire from another trench which he outflanked, and fell dying only a few feet from the enemy he had assaulted. A short time later a company of the Battalion attacked the enemy, who quickly surrendered. The devastating display of courage by Colonel Jones had completely undermined their will to fight further.

Thereafter the momentum of the attack was rapidly regained, Darwin and Goose Green were liberated, and the Battalion released the local inhabitants unharmed and forced the surrender of some 1,200 of the enemy.

The achievements of 2nd Battalion The Parachute Regiment at Darwin and Goose Green set the tone for the subsequent land victory on the Falklands. They achieved such a moral superiority over the enemy in this first battle that, despite the advantages of numbers and selection of battle-ground, they never thereafter doubted either the superior fighting qualities of the British troops, or their own inevitable defeat.

This was an action of the utmost gallantry by a Commanding Officer whose dashing leadership and courage throughout the battle were an inspiration to all about him.

---

Sergeant Ian John McKAY, The Parachute Regiment.

During the night of 11th/12th June 1982, 3rd Battalion The Parachute Regiment mounted a silent night attack on an enemy battalion position on Mount Longdon, an important objective in the battle for Port Stanley in the Falkland Islands. Sergeant McKay was platoon sergeant of 4 Platoon, B Company, which, after the initial objective had been secured, was ordered to clear the Northern side of the long East/West ridge feature, held by the enemy in depth, with strong, mutually-supporting positions. By now the enemy were fully alert, and resisting fiercely. As 4 Platoon's advance continued it came under increasingly heavy fire from a number of well-sited enemy machine gun positions on the ridge, and received casualties. Realising that no further advance was possible the Platoon Commander ordered the Platoon to move from its exposed position to seek shelter among the rocks of the ridge itself. Here it met up with part of 5 Platoon.

The enemy fire was still both heavy and accurate, and the position of the platoons was becoming increasingly hazardous. Taking Sergeant McKay, a Corporal and a few others, and covered by supporting machine gun fire, the Platoon Commander moved forward to reconnoitre the enemy positions but was hit by a bullet in the leg, and command devolved upon Sergeant McKay.

It was clear that instant action was needed if the advance was not to falter and increasing casualties to ensue. Sergeant McKay decided to convert this reconnaissance into an attack in order to eliminate the enemy positions. He was in no doubt of the strength and deployment of the enemy as he undertook this attack. He issued orders, and taking three men with him, broke cover and charged the enemy position.

The assault was met by a hail of fire. The Corporal was seriously wounded a Private killed and another wounded. Despite these losses Sergeant McKay, with complete disregard for his own safety, continued to charge the enemy position alone. On reaching it he despatched the enemy with grenades, thereby relieving the position of beleaguered 4 and 5 Platoons, who were now able to redeploy with relative safety. Sergeant McKay, however, was killed at the moment of victory, his body falling on the bunker.

Without doubt Sergeant McKay's action retrieved a most dangerous situation and was instrumental in ensuring the success of the attack. His was a coolly calculated act, the dangers of which must have been too apparent to him beforehand. Undeterred he performed with outstanding selflessness, perseverance and courage. With a complete disregard for his own safety, he displayed courage and leadership of the highest order, and was an inspiration to all those around him.

# NAVY DEPARTMENT
## LIFE PEER TO BE A BARON

Admiral of the Fleet Sir Terence LEWIN, G.C.B., M.V.O., D.S.C., Chief of the Defence Staff.

## DISTINGUISHED SERVICE ORDER

Commodore Samuel DUNLOP, C.B.E., Royal Fleet Auxiliary.
Captain Michael E. BARROW, Royal Navy.
Captain John J. BLACK, M.B.E., Royal Navy.
Captain William R. CANNING, Royal Navy.
Captain John F. COWARD, Royal Navy.
Captain Peter G. V. DINGEMANS, Royal Navy.
Captain Edmund S. J. LARKEN, Royal Navy.
Captain Christopher H. LAYMAN, M.V.O., Royal Navy.
Captain Linley E. MIDDLETON, A.D.C., Royal Navy.
Captain David PENTREATH, Royal Navy.
Captain Philip J. G. ROBERTS, Royal Fleet Auxiliary.
Lieutenant Colonel Nicholas F. VAUX, Royal Marines.
Lieutenant Colonel Andrew F. WHITEHEAD, Royal Marines.
Commander Christopher L. WREFORD-BROWN, Royal Navy.
Lieutenant Commander Brian F. DUTTON, Q.G.M., Royal Navy.

## DISTINGUISHED SERVICE CROSS
### (POSTHUMOUS)

Captain Ian H. NORTH, Merchant Navy.
Lieutenant Commander Gordon W. J. BATT, Royal Navy.
Lieutenant Commander John S. WOODHEAD, Royal Navy.
Lieutenant Commander John M. SEPHTON, Royal Navy.

## DISTINGUISHED SERVICE CROSS

Captain George R. GREEN, Royal Fleet Auxiliary.
Captain David E. LAWRENCE, Royal Fleet Auxiliary.
Captain Anthony F. PITT, Royal Fleet Auxiliary.
Commander Paul J. BOOTHERSTONE, Royal Navy.
Commander Christopher J. S. CRAIG, Royal Navy.
Commander Anthony MORTON, Royal Navy.
Commander Nicholas J. TOBIN, Royal Navy.
Commander Nigel D. WARD, A.F.C., Royal Navy.
Commander Alan W. J. WEST, Royal Navy.
Lieutenant Commander Andrew D. AULD, Royal Navy.
Lieutenant Commander Michael D. BOOTH, Royal Navy.
Lieutenant Commander Hugh S. CLARK, Royal Navy.
Lieutenant Commander Hugh J. LOMAS, Royal Navy.
Lieutenant Commander Neil W. THOMAS, Royal Navy.
Lieutenant Commander Simon C. THORNEWILL, Royal Navy.
Lieutenant Alan R. C. BENNETT, Royal Navy.
Lieutenant Nigel A. BRUEN, Royal Navy.
Lieutenant Richard HUTCHINGS, Royal Marines.
Lieutenant Nigel J. NORTH, Royal Navy.
Lieutenant Stephen R. THOMAS, Royal Navy.
Sub Lieutenant Peter T. MORGAN, Royal Navy.
Fleet Chief Petty Officer (Diver) Michael G. FELLOWS, B.E.M.

## MILITARY CROSS

Major Charles P. CAMERON, Royal Marines.
Captain Peter M. BABBINGTON, Royal Marines.
Lieutenant Clive I. DYTOR, Royal Marines.
Lieutenant Christopher FOX, Royal Marines.
Lieutenant David J. STEWART, Royal Marines.

## DISTINGUISHED FLYING CROSS
### (POSTHUMOUS)

Lieutenant Richard J. NUNN, Royal Marines.

## DISTINGUISHED FLYING CROSS

Captain Jeffrey P. NIBLETT, Royal Marines.

## AIR FORCE CROSS

Lieutenant Commander Douglas J. S. SQUIER, Royal Navy.
Lieutenant Commander Ralph J. S. WYKES-SNEYD, Royal Navy.

## DISTINGUISHED CONDUCT MEDAL

Corporal Julian BURDETT, Royal Marines.

## GEORGE MEDAL (POSTHUMOUS)

Second Engineer Officer Paul A. HENRY, Royal Fleet Auxiliary.

**Each man who received an award contributed to the eventual success of the operation. In this list space only allows us to reproduce one citation from the London Gazette for each of the three services.**

## GEORGE MEDAL

Able Seaman (Radar) John E. DILLON.

On 21st May 1982 Able Seaman (Radar) Dillon was in the After Damage Control Party onboard HMS ARDENT in Falkland Sound. Following a bomb attack on the ship he was assisting in the control of flooding in the Dining Hall when the area sustained further major bomb damage and he was rendered unconscious. On regaining consciousness he found that he was pinned to the deck by heavy debris in the dimly lit devastated compartment. A fire was raging and the area was rapidly filling with thick smoke.

He extricated himself and despite pain from a large shrapnel wound in his back attempted unsuccessfully to free a man pinned down by a girder across his neck. He then made his way through the smoke towards a further man calling for help, whom he found trapped under heavy metal girders, bleeding from head and face wounds and with his left hand severely damaged. After several attempts, between which he had to drop to the deck to get breathable air, AB Dillon succeeded in raising the debris sufficiently to allow the man to drag himself free. AB Dillon's antiflash hood had been ripped off in the explosion, so afforded him no protection from the heat, and his left ear was burned. In their search for an escape route, the man, who was heavily built, fell into a hole in the deck, but was dragged out by the much slighter AB Dillon to a hole in the ship's side where, although the man was able to inflate his own lifejacket, AB Dillon was unable to follow suit, due to the pain in his throat caused by the smoke. Despite this, fearing that the weakened man would be dragged beneath the ship, AB Dillon followed him into the water and pulled him away from the ship's side. By this time his exertions, pain and the cold of the sea had weakened AB Dillon until he could do little to support himself in the water. Realising that there was a danger of him pushing the man under the water if he continued to hold onto him, he moved away and appreciating that he could no longer swim or grasp the strop lowered to him from a helicopter, slipped beneath the surface. He and the man were then rescued by a helicopter crewman.

There is little doubt that but for Able Seaman (Radar) Dillon's selfless acts with complete disregard for his personal safety the other man would not have escaped from the ship which was then being abandoned and sinking.

## DISTINGUISHED SERVICE MEDAL
### (POSTHUMOUS)

Petty Officer Marine Engineering Mechanic (M) David R. BRIGGS
Acting Corporal Aircrewman Michael D. LOVE, Royal Marines.

## DISTINGUISHED SERVICE MEDAL

Colour Sergeant Michael J. FRANCIS, Royal Marines.
Chief Marine Engineering Mechanic (M) Michael D. TOWNSEND.
Chief Petty Officer (Diver) Graham M. TROTTER.
Chief Petty Officer Aircrewman Malcolm J. TUPPER.
Petty Officer John S. LEAKE.
Sergeant William J. LESLIE, Royal Marines.
Acting Petty Officer (Sonar) (SM) Graham J. R. LIBBY.
Leading Aircrewman Peter B. IMRIE.
Leading Seaman (Radar) Jeffrey D. WARREN.

## MILITARY MEDAL

Sergeant Thomas COLLINGS, Royal Marines.
Sergeant Michael COLLINS, Royal Marines.
Sergeant Joseph D. WASSELL, Royal Marines.
Corporal Michael ECCLES, Royal Marines.
Corporal David HUNT, Royal Marines.
Corporal Stephen C. NEWLAND, Royal Marines.
Corporal Harry SIDDALL, Royal Marines.
Corporal Chrystie N. H. WARD, Royal Marines.
Acting Corporal Andrew R. BISHOP, Royal Marines.
Marine Gary W. MARSHALL, Royal Marines.

# DISTINGUISHED FLYING MEDAL

Sergeant William C. O'BRIEN, Royal Marines.

## QUEEN'S GALLANTRY MEDAL
### (POSTHUMOUS)

Acting Colour Sergeant Brian JOHNSTON, Royal Marines.

Colour Sergeant Johnston, coxswain of LCU F4, was working in the vicinity of HMS ANTELOPE when her unexploded bomb detonated, starting an immediate fire which caused her crew, already at emergency stations, to be ordered to abandon ship. Without hesitation Colour Sergeant Johnston laid his craft alongside the ANTELOPE and began to fight the fire and take off survivors. At approximately 2200 he was ordered to stay clear of the ship because of the severity of the fire and the presence of a second unexploded bomb. Colour Sergeant Johnston remained alongside until his load was complete. In all LCU F4 rescued over 100 survivors from the ANTELOPE.

On 8 June, LCU F4 was attacked by enemy aircraft in Choiseul Sound. During this action Colour Sergeant Johnston and five of his crew were killed.

Colour Sergeant Johnston's selfless bravery in the face of extreme danger was in the highest traditions of the Corps.

## QUEEN'S GALLANTRY MEDAL

Chief Engineer Officer Charles K. A. ADAMS, Royal Fleet Auxiliary.
Lieutenant John K. BOUGHTON, Royal Navy.
Lieutenant Philip J. SHELDON, Royal Navy.
Third Officer Andrew GUDGEON, Royal Fleet Auxiliary.
Third Engineer Brian R. WILLIAMS, Merchant Navy.
Marine Engineering Artificer (M) 1st Class Kenneth ENTICKNAPP.
Petty Officer Medical Assistant Gerald A. MEAGER.

## MENTION IN DISPATCHES

Chief Officer J. K. BROCKLEHURST, Merchant Navy.
Commander R. D. FERGUSON, Royal Navy.
Chief Officer P. F. HILL, Royal Fleet Auxiliary.
Major P. R. LAMB, Royal Marines.
Commander R. C. LANE-NOTT, Royal Navy.
Commander T. M. LE MARCHAND, Royal Navy.
Major M. J. NORMAN, Royal Marines.
Major D. A. PENNEFATHER, Royal Marines.
Chief Engineer J. M. STEWART, Merchant Navy.
Commander J. B. TAYLOR, Royal Navy.
Commander B. G. TELFER, Royal Navy.
Major R. C. VAN DER HORST, Royal Marines.
Lieutenant Commander M. S. BLISSETT, Royal Navy.
Lieutenant Commander B. W. BRYANT, Royal Navy.
Lieutenant Commander R. G. BURROWS, Royal Navy.
Lieutenant Commander J. S. M. CHANDLER, Royal Navy.
Lieutenant Commander J. N. CLARK, Royal Navy.
Captain M. A. F. COLE, Royal Marines.
Lieutenant Commander G. R. A. CORYTON, Royal Navy.
Lieutenant Commander R. V. FREDERIKSEN, Royal Navy.
Lieutenant Commander D. G. GARWOOD, Royal Navy.
Lieutenant Commander A. C. GWILLIAM, Royal Navy.
Lieutenant Commander L. S. G. HULME, Royal Navy.
Lieutenant Commander I. INSKIP, Royal Navy.
Lieutenant Commander R. S. G. KENT, Royal Navy.
Lieutenant Commander J. A. LISTER, Royal Navy.
Lieutenant Commander I. B. MACKAY, Royal Navy.
Lieutenant Commander C. R. W. MORRELL, Royal Navy.
Lieutenant Commander K. M. NAPIER, Royal Navy.
Captain A. B. NEWCOMBE, Royal Marines.
Lieutenant Commander M. J. O'CONNELL, Royal Navy.
Captain E. J. O'KANE, Royal Marines.
Captain A. R. PILLAR, Royal Marines.
Captain N. E. POUNDS, Royal Marines.
Lieutenant Commander A. A. RICH, Royal Navy.
Lieutenant Commander R. E. WILKINSON, Royal Navy.
Lieutenant P. J. BARBER, Royal Navy.
Lieutenant N. A. M. BUTLER, Royal Navy.
Lieutenant C. T. G. CAROE, Royal Marines.
Lieutenant C. H. T. CLAYTON, Royal Navy.
Lieutenant R. L. CRAWFORD, Royal Marines.
Lieutenant W. A. CURTIS, Royal Navy (Posthumous).
Lieutenant A. J. EBBENS, Royal Marines.

Lieutenant W. J. T. FEWTRELL, Royal Marines.
Lieutenant F. HADDOW, Royal Marines.
Lieutenant R. I. HORTON, Royal Navy.
Lieutenant H. J. LEDINGHAM, Royal Navy.
Lieutenant D. A. LORD, Royal Navy.
Lieutenant P. C. MANLEY, Royal Navy.
Lieutenant A. N. McHARG, Royal Navy.
Lieutenant J. A. G. MILLER, Royal Navy.
Lieutenant P. G. MILLER, Royal Navy.
Lieutenant A. G. MOLL, Royal Navy.
Lieutenant R. J. ORMSHAW, Royal Navy.
Lieutenant C. L. PALMER, Royal Navy.
Lieutenant R. F. PLAYFORD, Royal Marines.
Lieutenant C. J. POLLARD, Royal Navy.
Lieutenant A. PRINGLE, Royal Navy.
Lieutenant P. I. M. RAINEY, Royal Navy.
Lieutenant F. W. ROBERTSON, Royal Navy.
Lieutenant R. E. J. SLEEMAN, Royal Navy.
Lieutenant D. A. B. SMITH, Royal Navy.
Lieutenant N. TAYLOR, Royal Navy (Posthumous).
Lieutenant C. TODHUNTER, Royal Navy.
Sub Lieutenant R. J. BARKER, Royal Navy.
Sub Lieutenant R. C. EMLY, Royal Navy (Posthumous).
Sub Lieutenant D. E. GRAHAM, Royal Navy.
Sub Lieutenant P. J. HUMPHREYS, Royal Navy.
Midshipman M. T. FLETCHER, Royal Navy.
Fleet Chief Marine Engineering Artificer (P) E. M. UREN.
Warrant Officer Class 2 R. J. BROWN, Royal Marines.
Warrant Officer Class 2 A. S. ROBINSON, Royal Marines.
Chief Air Engineering Artificer (M) R. J. BENTLEY.
Marine Engineering Artificer (H) 1st Class D. A. BUGDEN.
Colour Sergeant B. DAVIES, Royal Marines.
Weapon Engineering Artificer 1st Class A. C. EGGINGTON (Posthumous)
Chief Marine Engineering Artificer (H) K. W. GOLDIE.
Chief Petty Officer (Ops) (M) E. GRAHAM.
Chief Petty Officer (Diver) B. T. GUNNELL.
Marine Engineering Artificer (H) 1st Class P. G. JAKEMAN.
Marine Engineering Artificer (M) 1st Class K. S. LAKE.
Chief Petty Officer Airman (AH) N. C. MARTIN.
Marine Engineering Mechaniciam (M) 1st Class T. MILES.
Marine Engineering Artificer (M) 1st Class S. D. MITCHELL.
Weapon Engineering Mechanician 1st Class P. R. MOIR.
Marine Engineering Mechanician (M) 1st Class H. B. PORTER.
Marine Engineering Mechanician 1st Class A. G. SIDDLE.
Chief Marine Engineering Mechanic T. G. SMITH.
Marine Engineering Artificer (M) 1st Class S. P. TARABELLA.
Acting Chief Weapon Engineering Mechanician M. G. TILL. (Posthumous).
Marine Engineering Mechanician (L) 1st Class W. G. WADDINGTON.
Colour Sergeant E. YOUNG, Royal Marines.
Petty Officer Aircrewman A. ASHDOWN.
Petty Officer Aircrewman J. A. BALLS, B.E.M.
Sergeant P. BEEVERS, Royal Marines.
Sergeant I. W. BRICE, Royal Marines.
Sergeant E. L. BUCKLEY, Royal Marines.
Sergeant B. G. BURGESS, Royal Marines.
Petty Officer Aircrewman R. BURNETT.
Sergeant E. R. CANDLISH, Royal Marines.
Sergeant R. T. COOPER, Royal Marines.
Sergeant G. DANCE, Royal Marines.
Sergeant C. C. DE LA COUR, Q.G.M. Royal Marines.
Sergeant B. DOLIVERA, Royal Marines.
Petty Officer Marine Engineering Mechanic (M) J. R. ELLIS.
Sergeant A. P. EVANS, Royal Marines, (Posthumous).
Sergeant I. D. FISK, Royal Marines.
Weapons Engineering Artificer 2nd Class J. M. C. FOY.
Sergeant D. K. HADLOW, Royal Marines.
Sergeant K. M. JAMES, Q.G.M., Royal Marines.
Petty Officer (Missile) H. JONES.
Marine Engineering Artificer 2nd Class D. J. LEANING.
Sergeant W. D. P. LEWIS, Royal Marines.
Sergeant M. McINTYRE, Royal Marines.
Sergeant H. F. NAPIER, Royal Marines.
Petty Officer Air Engineering Mechanic (M) S. RAINSBURY.
Acting Petty Officer Marine Engineering Mechanic (M) D. M. K. ROSS.
Sergeant T. A. SANDS, Royal Marines.
Sergeant W. J. STOCKS, Royal Marines.

Sergeant C. R. STONE, Royal Marines.
Petty Officer Aircrewman C. W. TATTERSALL.
Weapon Engineering Mechanician 2nd Class B. J. WALLIS (Posthumous).
Sergeant R. D. WRIGHT, Royal Marines.
Acting Leading Medical Assistant G. BLACK.
Acting Leading Marine Engineering Mechanic (M) C. R. BOSWELL.
Corporal C. J. G. BROWN, Royal Marines.
Corporal G. COOKE, Royal Marines.
Leading Seaman (Missile) R. M. GOULD.
Leading Aircrewman J. A. HARPER.
Acting Leading Marine Engineering Mechanic (M) S. W. HATHAWAY.
Leading Radio Operator (Tactical) R. J. HUTCHESON.
Leading Seaman (Diver) P. M. KEARNS.
Corporal T. W. McMAHON, Royal Marines.
Leading Aircrewman I. ROBERTSON.
Leading Seaman (Diver) C. A. SMITHARD.
Leading Seaman (Diver) A. S. THOMPSON.
Leading Aircrewman S. W. WRIGHT.
Leading Medical Assistant P. YOUNGMAN.
Radio Operator (Tactical) 1st Class, R. J. ASH.
Lance Corporal P. W. BOORN, Royal Marines.
Able Seaman (Missile) N. S. BROTHERTON.
Marine Engineering Mechanic (M) 1st Class L. CARTWRIGHT.
Marine Engineering Mechanic (M) 1st Class M. L. CHIPLEN.
Able Seaman (Missile) A. COPPELL.
Marine Engineering Mechanic (M) 1st Class C. CROWLEY.
Marine Engineering Mechanic (M) 1st Class D. J. EDWARDS.
Lance Corporal B. GILBERT, Royal Marines.
Able Seaman (Missile) S. INGLEBY.
Able Seaman (Radar) M. S. LEACH.
Medical Assistant M. NICELY.
Marine Engineering Mechanic (M) 1st Class D. J. SERRELL.
Marine Engineering Mechanic (M) 1st Class A. STEWART.
Able Seaman (Diver) D. WALTON.
Marine R. BAINBRIDGE, Royal Marines.
Marine N. J. BARNETT, Royal Marines.
Marine D. S. COMBES, Royal Marines.
Marine G. CUTHELL, Royal Marines.
Marine L. DANIELS, Royal Marines.
Marine S. DUGGAN, Royal Marines.
Marine L. J. GOLDSMITH, Royal Marines.
Marine G. HODKINSON, Royal Marines.
Marine M. A. NEAT, Royal Marines.
Marine G. NORDASS, Royal Marines.
Marine D. L. O'CONNOR, Royal Marines.
Marine C. J. SCRIVENER, Royal Marines.
Marine J. STONESTREET, Royal Marines.
Marine R. S. STRANGE, Royal Marines.
Marine P. THOMASON, Royal Marines.
Seaman (OPS) D. J. WHILD.
Marine P. K. WILSON, Royal Marines.

## QUEEN'S COMMENDATION FOR BRAVE CONDUCT

Second Officer I. POVEY, Royal Fleet Auxiliary.
Chief Marine Engineering Mechanic (L) A. F. FAZACKERLEY.
Chief Weapon Engineering Mechanic (R) W. RUMSEY.
Weapon Engineering Mechanic (R) 1st Class J. R. JESSON.
Marine Engineering Mechanician (M) 1st Class T. A. SUTTON.
Acting Colour Sergeant D. A. WATKINS, Royal Marines.
Petty Officer Class 2 B. CZARNECKI, Merchant Navy.
Petty Officer Weapon Engineering Mechanic (R) G. J. LOWDEN.
Radio Operator (Tactical) 1st Class D. F. SULLIVAN.
Marine P. A. CRUDEN, Royal Marines.

# ARMY DEPARTMENT
## DISTINGUISHED SERVICE ORDER

Major Cedric N. G. DELVES, The Devonshire and Dorset Regiment.
Major Christopher P. B. KEEBLE, The Parachute Regiment.
Lieutenant Colonel Hew W. R. PIKE, M.B.E., The Parachute Regiment.
Lieutenant Colonel Michael I. E. SCOTT, Scots Guards.

## DISTINGUISHED SERVICE CROSS

Warrant Officer Class 2 John H. PHILLIPS, Corps of Royal Engineers.

## MILITARY CROSS (POSTHUMOUS)

Captain Gavin J. HAMILTON, The Green Howards.

## MILITARY CROSS

Major Michael H. ARGUE, The Parachute Regiment.
Captain Timothy W. BURLS, The Parachute Regiment.
Major David A. COLLETT, The Parachute Regiment.
Lieutenant Colin S. CONNOR, The Parachute Regiment.
Major John H. CROSLAND, The Parachute Regiment.
Major Charles D. FARRAR-HOCKLEY, The Parachute Regiment.
Major John P. KISZELY, Scots Guards.
Lieutenant Robert A. D. LAWRENCE, Scots Guards.
Captain William A. McCRACKEN, Royal Regiment of Artillery.
Captain Aldwin J. G. WIGHT, Welsh Guards.

## DISTINGUISHED FLYING CROSS

Captain Samuel M. DRENNAN, Army Air Corps.
Captain John G. GREENHALGH, Royal Corps of Transport.

## DISTINGUISHED CONDUCT MEDAL (POSTHUMOUS)

Private Stephen ILLINGSWORTH, The Parachute Regiment.
Guardsman James B. C. REYNOLDS, Scots Guards.

## DISTINGUISHED CONDUCT MEDAL

Corporal David ABOLS, The Parachute Regiment.
Staff Sergeant Brian FAULKNER, The Parachute Regiment.
Sergeant John C. MEREDITH, The Parachute Regiment.
Warrant Officer Class 2 William NICOL, Scots Guards.
Sergeant John S. PETTINGER, The Parachute Regiment.

## CONSPICUOUS GALLANTRY MEDAL (POSTHUMOUS)

Staff Sergeant James PRESCOTT, Corps of Royal Engineers.

## MILITARY MEDAL (POSTHUMOUS)

Private Richard J. de M. ABSOLON, The Parachute Regiment.
Lance Corporal Gary D. BINGLEY, The Parachute Regiment.

## MILITARY MEDAL

Corporal Ian P. BAILEY, The Parachute Regiment.
Lance Corporal Stephen A. BARDSLEY, The Parachute Regiment.
Sergeant Terence I. BARRETT, The Parachute Regiment.
Lance Corporal Martin W. L. BENTLEY, The Parachute Regiment.
Sergeant Derrick S. BOULTBY, Royal Corps of Transport.
Corporal Trevor BROOKES, Royal Corps of Signals.
Corporal Brookes commanded a 4 man patrol tasked to provide vital information on enemy dispositions and installations on East Falklands as prelude to the repossession of the islands.
Inserted by helicopter from the Naval Task Force at a distance of 120 miles from the islands, he maintained observation of the Darwin/Goose Green area for a period of 16 days. His position was most vulnerable at all times as the difficulty of achieving observation on the target necessitated him surviving under the main enemy helicopter route between Stanley and Darwin. Frequent enemy air searches and foot patrols were carried out in the area. He fully realised that no support was available to him, in the event of compromise by enemy action. His courage and leadership in this situation was of the highest order.
The accuracy of his reporting was such that a successful air strike was carried out on his information, against a petrol installation on the airfield at Goose Green. His information was of great value during the preparation for the successful attack on Darwin/Goose Green by 2nd Battalion The Parachute Regiment.
His performance as an individual and a leader was in the highest traditions of his Regiment and the Army as a whole.
Corporal Thomas J. CAMP, The Parachute Regiment.
Private Graham S. CARTER, The Parachute Regiment.
Guardsman Stephen M. CHAPMAN, Welsh Guards.
Corporal John A. FORAN, Corps of Royal Engineers.
Sergeant D. FULLER, The Parachute Regiment.
Private Barry J. GRAYLING, The Parachute Regiment.
Corporal Thomas W. HARLEY, The Parachute Regiment.

Bombadier Edward M. HOLT, Royal Regiment of Artillery.
Sergeant Robert W. JACKSON, Scots Guards.
Lance Corporal Dale J. LOVERIDGE, Welsh Guards.
Sergeant Joseph G. MATHER, Special Air Service Regiment.
Sergeant Peter H. R. NAYA, Royal Army Medical Corps.
Warrant Officer Class 2 Brian T. NECK, Welsh Guards.
Guardsman Andrew S. PENGELLY, Scots Guards.
Lance Corporal Leslie J. L. STANDISH, The Parachute Regiment.
Sergeant Roman H. WREGA, Corps of Royal Engineers.

# MENTIONED IN DESPATCHES

Sergeant I. AIRD, The Parachute Regiment.
Private S. J. ALEXANDER, The Parachute Regiment.
Lieutenant Colonel J. ANDERSON, Royal Army Medical Corps.
Corporal R. E. ARMSTRONG, The Royal Greenjackets (Posthumous)
Major The Honourable R. N. BETHEL, M.B.E., Scots Guards.
Captain A. P. BOURNE, Royal Regiment of Artillery.
Private A. E. BROOKE, The Parachute Regiment.
Driver M. BROUGH, Royal Corps of Transport.
Captain C. C. BROWN, Royal Regiment of Artillery.
Guardsman G. BROWN, Scots Guards.
Captain I. A. BRYDEN, Scots Guards.
Major W. K. BUTLER, Royal Corps of Signals.
Staff Sergeant W.H. CARPENTER Special Air Service
Lance Corporal L.A. CARVER, The Parachute Regiment
Lieutenant (Queen's Gurkha Officer) CHANDRAKUMAR PRADHAN, 7th Duke of Edinburgh's Own Gurkha Rifles
Staff Sergeant T. COLLINS, Corps of Royal Engineers
Private K.P. CONNERY, The Parachute Regiment
Chaplain to the Forces Third Class D. COOPER, Royal Army Chaplain's Department
Lieutenant M.R. CORETH, The Blues and Royals
Private A.M. CORNEILLE, The Parachute Regiment
Corporal I.C. CORRIGAN, Corps of Royal Electrical and Mechanical Engineers
Lieutenant M.T. COX, The Parachute Regiment
Staff Sergeant P.P. CURRASS, Q.G.M., Royal Army Medical Corps (Posthumos)
Lance Sergeant A.C.E. DALGLEISH, Scots Guards
Lance Corporal N.J. DANCE, The Parachute Regiment
Lance Sergeant I. DAVIDSON, Scots Guards
Major P.E. DENNISON, The Parachute Regiment
Staff Sergeant G.K. DIXON, Royal Regiment of Artillery
Piper S.W. DUFFY, Scots Guards
Lance Corporal K.P. DUNBAR, The Parachute Regiment
Gunner G. ECCLESTON, Royal Regiment of Artillery
Captain M.P. ENTWISTLE, Royal Army Medical Corps
Lieutenant Colonel K.R.H. EVE, Royal Regiment of Artillery
Captain P.R. FARRAR, The Parachute Regiment
Private M.W. FLETCHER, The Parachute Regiment (Posthumous)
Corporal D. FORD, Corps of Royal Engineers
Warrant Officer Class 2, J.F. FRANCIS, Royal Regiment of Artillery
Lieutenant D.P. FRANKLAND, Royal Corps of Transport
Lance Corporal ROY GILLON, Corps of Royal Engineers
Private D.J. GOUGH, The Parachute Regiment
Lance Serjeant D. GRAHAM, Welsh Guards
Private D. GRAY, The Parachute Regiment
Major P.H. GULLAN, M.B.E., M.C., The Parachute Regiment
Acting Corporal J.E. HAND, The Parachute Regiment
Acting Corporal S.P. HARDING-DEMPSTER, The Parachute Regiment
Corporal D. HARDMAN, The Parachute Regiment (Posthumous)
Private P.J. HARLEY, The Parachute Regiment
Major R.B. HAWKEN, Corps of Royal Engineers
Lieutenant R.C. HENDICOTT, Corps of Royal Engineers
Acting Sergeant J. HILL, The Parachute Regiment
Lieutentant Colonel G.A. HOLT, Royal Regiment of Artillery
Warrant Officer Class 2, G. HOUGH, Welsh Guards
Captain E.H. HOUSTOUN, M.B.E., Grenadier Guards
Acting Bombardier O.D. HUGHES, Royal Regiment of Artillery
Captain S.J. HUGHES, Royal Army Medical Corps

Corporal S.D. ILES, Corps of Royal Engineers
Lieutenant The Lord R.A. INNES-KER, The Blues and Royals
Bombardier J.R. JACKSON, Royal Regiment of Artillery
Gunner J. JONES, Royal Regiment of Artillery
Lance Corporal K.B. JONES, Royal Corps of Transport
Sergeant R.R. KALINSKI, The Parachute Regiment
Captain S.J. KNAPPER, The Staffordshire Regiment
Acting Warrant Officer Class 2, A. LA FRENAIS, Special Air Service Regiment
Major B.C. LAMBE, Royal Regiment of Artillery
Lieutenant C.R. LIVINGSTONE, Corps of Royal Engineers
Lance Corporal C.K. LOVETT, The Parachute Regiment (Posthumous)
Lieutenant J.G.O. LOWE, Royal Corps of Transport
Staff Sergeant C.D. LOWTHER, Special Air Service Regiment
Lance Corporal D. MACCOLL, Scots Guards
Major R. MACDONALD, Corps of Royal Engineers
Piper P.A. MACINNES, Scots Guards
Lance Corporal J.D. MAHER, Corps of Royal Engineers
Captain R.J. MAKEIG-JONES, Royal Regiment of Artillery
Private A. MANSFIELD, The Parachute Regiment
Major T.A. MARSH, The Parachute Regiment
Sergeant P.J. MARSHALL, Army Catering Corps
Lance Sergeant T. McGUINNESS, Scots Guards
Captain J.H. McMANNERS, Royal Regiment of Artillery
Lieutenant A.M. MITCHELL, Scots Guards
Lance Sergeant C. MITCHELL, Scots Guards (Posthumous)
2nd Lieutenant I.C. MOORE, The Parachute Regiment
Private R.P.G. MORRELL, The Parachute Regiment
Major P. NEAME, The Parachute Regiment
Corporal T.K. NOBLE, The Parachute Regiment
Private E. O'ROURKE, The Parachute Regiment
Lieutenant J.D. PAGE, The Parachute Regiment
Acting Corporal D.J. PEARCY, Intelligence Corps
Corporal J.F. PHILLIPS, The Parachute Regiment
Private (Acting Sergeant) B.W. PITCHFORTH, The Queen's Regiment
Private A. POTTER, Royal Army Ordnance Corps
Lance Corporal B.J. RANDALL, Corps of Royal Engineers
Sergeant P. RATCLIFFE, Special Air Service Regiment
Lance Corporal G. RENNIE, Scots Guards
Warrant Officer Class 2, M.D. RICHARDS, Royal Regiment of Artillery
Lance Corporal J.J. RIGG, Army Air Corps
Lieutenant Colonel J.D.A. ROBERTS, Royal Army Medical Corps
Major B.P.S. ROLFE-SMITH, The Parachute Regiment
Captain C.R. ROMBERG, Royal Regiment of Artillery
Lieutenant Colonel H. M. ROSE, O.B.E., Coldstream Guards
Sergeant I. ROY, Corps of Royal Engineers
Captain J.D.G. SAYERS, Welsh Guards
Acting Captain M.R SELFRIDGE, The Parachute Regiment (Posthumous)
Warrant Officer Class 2 M.J. SHARP, Army Air Corps
Corporal J.W. SIBLEY, The Parachute Regiment
Major C.S. SIBUN, Army Air Corps
Acting Lance Corporal W.A. SKINNER, Corps of Royal Engineers
Major G.F.W. SMITH, Royal Regiment of Artillery
Captain R.J. SOUTHWORTH, Royal Army Ordnance Corps
Corporal of Horse P. STRETTON, The Blues and Royals
2nd Lieutenant J.D. STUART, Scots Guards
Lieutenant W.J. SYMS, Welsh Guards
Acting Sergeant R.C. TAYLOR, Royal Corps of Signals
Major A. TODD, Royal Corps of Transport
Lance Corporal G. TYTLER, Scots Guards
Acting Corporal P.A. WALKER, The Staffordshire Regiment
Sergeant R.J. WALKER, Army Air Corps
2nd Lieutenant G. WALLIS, The Parachute Regiment
Lieutenant M.E. WARING, Royal Regiment of Artillery
Captain J.N.E. WATSON, Royal Regiment of Artillery
Lieutenant G.R. WEIGHELL, The Parachute Regiment
Lieutenant M.G. WILLIAMS, Royal Regiment of Artillery
Lieutenant M.S.H. WORSLEY-TONKS, The Parachute Regiment

# AIR FORCE DEPARTMENT
## DISTINGUISHED SERVICE CROSS
Flight Lieutenant David H.S. MORGAN, Royal Air Force, 899 Naval Air Squadron

## DISTINGUISHED FLYING CROSS
Wing Commander Peter T. SQUIRE AFC, Royal Air Force
Squadron Leader Richard U. LANGWORTHY AFC, Royal Air Force

Squadron Leader Langworthy was onboard MV NORLAND and latterly HMS FEARLESS anchored in San Carlos Water during the period 21st-26th May 1982. On 25th May, MV ATLANTIC CONVEYOR was hit and destroyed by an enemy attack. All of No. 18 Squadron's assets, less one Chinook helicopter, were destroyed. This remaining aircraft ZA 718 was flown to San Carlos Water. A small detachment under the command of Squadron Leader Langworthy was put ashore on 27th May to operate this one aircraft in support of land and sea operations. The Detachment possessed no field deployment equipment and operated initially from "fox holes". Permanent accommodation and messing were subsequently established at Port San Carlos Settlement. Despite a total lack of aircraft spares, ZA 718 was flown continuously in support of the battle from 27th May until the cease fire. On 30th May, Squadron Leader Langworthy was briefed to move 3 x 105 mm light guns (two internal plus one external), 85 men and 22 tonnes of ammunition to Mount Kent. The move was to take place at night using Passive Night Goggles Techniques. The intelligence briefing was vague, but it was assessed that the enemy was in position on Mount Kent and additionally had Company positions at Estancia House. The first load of 3 x 105 mm light guns plus 22 men took 2½ hours to load. The transit proved uneventful despite severe snow showers in the area. The drop point briefed as a flat plateau, proved to be a sloping rock river with flattish areas and adjacent deep gullies. Full operation of the rear cabin ramp proved difficult over such terrain and the off-loading took 40 minutes. This was achieved without lights and further complicated by intercom failure on the aircraft. While not directly engaged by enemy fire, the general area in which the aircraft had landed was subject to fire. On completion of the off-loading the aircraft was recovered in appalling weather conditions of heavy snow. The aircraft radio altimeter failed and the aircraft struck the sea causing some minor damage. Squadron Leader Langworthy recovered this situation and the aircraft was recovered to its operating base without further mishap.

Squadron Leader Calum N. McDOUGALL, Royal Air Force
Squadron Leader Jeremy J. POOK, Royal Air Force
Flight Lieutenant William F.M. WITHERS, Royal Air Force

## AIR FORCE CROSS
Wing Commander David EMMERSON, Royal Air Force
Squadron Leader Robert TUXFORD, Royal Air Force
Flight Lieutenant Harold C. BURGOYNE, Royal Air Force

## QUEEN'S GALLANTRY MEDAL
Flight Lieutenant Alan J. SWAN, Royal Air Force
Flight Sergeant Brian W. JOPLING, Royal Air Force

## MENTIONED IN DESPATCHES
Squadron Leader J.G. ELLIOTT, Royal Air Force
Squdron Leader R.D. IVESON, Royal Air Force
Flight Lieutenant E.H. BALL, Royal Air Force
Flight Lieutenant M.W.J. HARE, Royal Air Force
Flight Lieutenant G.C. GRAHAM, Royal Air Force
Flight Lieutenant A.T. JONES, Royal Air Force
Flight Lieutenant I. MORTIMER, Royal Air Force
Flight Lieutenant H. PRIOR, Royal Air Force
Flight Lieutenant R.J. RUSSELL, A.F.C., Royal Air Force
Flight Lieutenant R.D. WRIGHT, Royal Air Force
Flying Officer P.L. TAYLOR, Royal Air Force
Flying Officer C. MILLER, Royal Air Force
Flight Sergeant D.W. KNIGHTS, Royal Air Force
Corporal A.D. TOMLINSON, Royal Air Force

## QUEEN'S COMMENDATION FOR BRAVE CONDUCT
Junior Technician A. THORNE, Royal Air Force
Senior Aircraftman K.J. SOPPETT-MOSS, Royal Air Force

# ORDER OF THE BATH (MILITARY DIVISION)
## K.C.B.
Major General John J. MOORE, C.B., O.B.E., M.C. *
Rear Admiral John F. WOODWARD

## C.B.
Air Vice-Marshal George A. CHESWORTH, O.B.E., D.F.C., Royal Air Force
Commodore Michael C. CLAPP, Royal Navy
Air Vice-Marshall Kenneth W. HAYR, C.B.E., A.F.C., Royal Air Force
Brigadier Julian H.A. THOMPSON, O.B.E., A.D.C., Royal Marines
Rear Admiral Anthony J. WHETSTONE

# ORDER OF THE BRITISH EMPIRE (MILITARY DIVISION)
## G.B.E.
Admiral Sir John D.E. FIELDHOUSE, G.C.B.

## K.B.E.
Air Marshal Sir John B. CURTISS, K.C.B., Royal Air Force
Vice Admiral David J. HALLIFAX

## C.B.E
Captain Paul BADCOCK, Royal Navy
Captain Nicholas J. BARKER, Royal Navy
Colonel Ian S. BAXTER, M.B.E.
Colonel John D. BIDMEAD, O.B.E.
Captain Christopher P.O. BURNE, Royal Navy
Colonel David B.H. COLLEY, O.B.E.
Group Captain Clive E. EVANS, Royal Air Force
Captain Raymond H. FOX, Royal Navy
Captain John GARNIER, M.V.O., Royal Navy
Group Captain Alexander F.C. HUNTER, O.B.E., A.F.C., Royal Air Force
Group Captain Patrick KING, O.B.E., Royal Air Force
Captain Michael H.G. LAYARD, Royal Navy
Colonel Bruce C. McDERMOTT, O.B.E.
Captain Robert McQUEEN, Royal Navy
Group Captain Jeremy S.B. PRICE, A.D.C., Royal Air Force
Captain Jonathan J.R. TOD, Royal Navy
Captain John P. WRIGLEY, Royal Navy

# ORDER OF THE BRITISH EMPIRE (CIVIL DIVISION)
## C.B.E
Captain Donald A. ELLERBY, Master, M.V. NORLAND
Captain Dennis J. SCOTT-MASSON, Master, SS CANBERRA
Captain John P. MORTON, Master, M.V. ELK

## O.B.E.
Captain William J.C. CLARKE, Master, M.V. EUROPIC FERRY
Captain Alan FULTON, Master, Cable Ship IRIS
Captain David M. RUNDLE, Master, M.V. BRITISH WYE
Captain Michael J. SLACK, Master, M.S. WIMPEY SEA-HORSE

# BRITISH EMPIRE MEDAL (CIVIL DIVISION)
Garry BALES, Able Seaman, Tug IRISHMAN
Richard BARRETT, Chief Steward, Cable Ship IRIS
Dennis P. BETTS, Able Seaman, Tug IRISHMAN
James A. GOLDIE, Stores Officer, Royal Fleet Auxiliary RESOURCE
Jack JOHNSTON, Senior Storekeeper, Royal Fleet Auxiliary FORT AUSTIN
Alan J. LEONARD, Chief Cook, SS ATLANTIC CAUSEWAY
Paul McEWAN, Stores Officer, Royal Fleet Auxiliary REGENT

# LEST WE FORGET . . .

HMS Antelope

Ships and equipment will eventually be replaced. This book is dedicated to all the men who made the supreme sacrifice during the conflict . . .

Private Richard Absolon
Petty Officer Michael Adcock
Air Eng Mech Adrian Anslow
Mne Eng Mech Frank Armes
Able Seaman Derek Armstrong
Rifleman Raymond Armstrong
Sergeant John Arthy
WO2 Malcolm Atkinson
Staff Sgt John Baker
Lt Commander Richard Banfield RN
Able Seaman Andrew Barr
Lieutenant James Barry
Lt Commander Gordon Batt
Corporal William Begley
L/Corporal Gary Bingley
Able Seaman Ian Boldy
Petty Officer Peter Brouard
Private Gerald Bull
L/Corporal Barry Bullers
Corporal Paul Bunker
L/Corporal Anthony Burke
Corporal Robert Burns
Private Jason Burt
Chief Petty Officer John Caddy
Marine Paul Callan
Mne Eng Art Paul Callus
L/Sergeant James Carlyle
Bosun Chee Yu Sik
L/Corporal Simon Cockton
Private Albert Connett
L/Corporal Anthony Cork
Private Jonathan Crow
Sergeant Philip Currass
Guardsman Ian Dale
Sergeant Sid Davidson
Marine Colin Davison
A/Petty Officer Stephen Dawson
Guardsman Derek Denholm
Captain Christopher Dent
Elect Fitter Dis Leung Chau
Private Stephen Dixon
A/Wpns Eng Mech John Dobson
Private Mark Dodsworth
Cook Richard Dunkerley
Guardsman Michael Dunphy
Butcher Dis Sung Yuk Fai
Cook Brian Easton
Sergeant Clifford Elley
Sergeant Roger Enefer
Sergeant Andrew Evans
Corporal Kenneth Evans

Guardsman Peter Edwards
L/Corporal Ian Farrell
C/Sergeant Gordon Findlay
Corporal Peter Fitton
Chief Petty Officer Edmund Flanagan
Private Mark Fletcher
A/Ldg Cook Michael Foote
Mar Eng Mech Stephen Ford
Major Michael Forge
Petty Officer Michael Fowler
Lieutenant Kenneth Francis
WO2 Laurence Gallagher
Sapper Pradeep Gandhi
Guardsman Mark Gibby
Guardsman Glenn Grace
Guardsman Paul Green
Private Anthony Greenwood
L/Corporal Brett Giffen
S/Sergeant Christopher Griffen
Marine Robert Griffin
Guardsman Gareth Griffiths
Private Neil Grose
3rd Eng Officer Christopher Hailwood RFA
Wpns Eng Mech Ian Hall
Captain Gavin Hamilton
A/Steward Shaun Hanson
Corporal David Hardman
Corporal William Hatton
Flt Lieutenant Garth Hawkins RAF
Able Seaman Sean Hayward
Lieutenant Rodney Heath RN
Air Eng Mech Mark Henderson
2nd Eng Officer Paul Henry RFA
Able Seaman Stephen Heyes
L/Corporal Peter Higgs
Air Eng Mech Brian Hinge
Chief Radio Officer Ronald Hoole
Corporal Stephen Hope
Guardsman Denis Hughes
Guardsman Gareth Hughes
Sergeant William Hughes
A/Sergeant Ian Hunt
Private Peter Hedicker
Private Stephen Illingsworth
Mne Eng Art Alexander James
Guardsman Brian Jasper
Private Timothy Jenkins
C/Sergeant Brian Johnston
Sapper Christopher Jones
Private Craig Jones
Private Michael Jones

Lieut Colonel Herbert Jones
Corporal Philip Jones
Sailor Kam Yung Shui
Guardsman Anthony Keeble
L/Sergeant Kevin Keoghane
Laundryman Kyo Ben Kwo
Private Stewart Laing
Wpns Eng Mech Simon Lawson
Chief Petty Officer David Lee
Sergeant Robert Leeming
Marine Eng Mech Alistair Leighton
L/Corporal Paul Lightfoot
Corporal Michael Love
L/Corporal Christopher Lovett
Corporal Douglas MacCormack
Marine Gordon Macpherson
Cook Brian Malcolm
Guardsman David Malcolmson
Guardsman Michael Marks
Naval Airman Brian Marsden
Marine Stephen McAndrews
Corporal Keith McCarthy
Air Eng Art Kelvin McCullum
Corporal Michael McHugh
Sergeant Ian McKay
L/Corporal Peter McKay
Corporal Stewart McLaughlin
Corporal Andrew McIlvenny
Air Eng Mech Allan McAuley
Private Thomas Mechan
Corporal Michael Melia
Private Richard Middlewick
A/Ldg Mne Mech David Miller
L/Sergeant Clark Mitchell
Guardsman Christopher Mordecai
3rd Eng Off Andrew Morris RFA
A/Ldg Seaman Michael Mullen
L/Corporal James Murdoch
Lieutenant Brian Murphy RN
Ldg P.T. Inst Gary Nelson
L/Corporal Stephen Newbury
Corporal John Newton
Guardsman Gareth Nicholson
Marine Michael Nowak
Lieut Richard Nunn RM
Major Roger Nutbeam RAMC
Staff Sgt Patrick O'Connor
A/Wpns Eng Mech David Ozbirn
A/Petty Officer Andrew Palmer
Private David Parr
Guardsman Colin Parsons

119

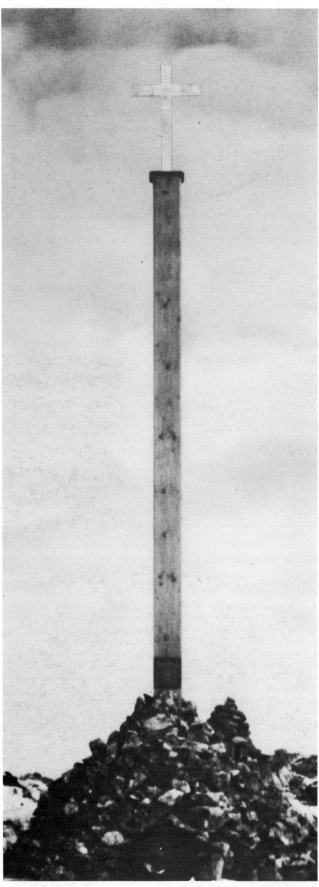

The permanent memorial made by the men of Stena Seaspread and erected, overlooking San Carlos, in memory of the men onboard HMS Ardent and Antelope.

L/Corporal John Pashley
Mne Eng Mech Terence Perkins
Guardsman Eirwyn Phillips
Marine Keith Phillips
Seaman Po Ng
Guardsman Gareth Poole
Staff Sergeant James Prescott
Private Kenneth Preston
Corporal Stephen Prior
L/Air Eng Mech Donald Pryce
Guardsman James Reynolds
Cook John Roberts
Lt Commander Glen Robinson-Moltke RN
Craftsman Mark Rollins
Sergeant Ronald Rotherham
Guardsman Nigel Rowberry
Marine Anthony Rundle
L/Cook Mark Sambles
L/Corporal David Scott
Private Ian Scrivens
Lt Commander John Sephton RN
Craftsman Alexander Shaw
Seaman Shing Chan Chai
L/Cook Anthony Sillence
Sergeant John Simeon
Private Francis Slough
Corporal Jeremy Smith
Private Mark Holman-Smith
L/Corporal Nigel Smith
Corporal Ian Spencer
L/Radio Op Bernard Still
Guardsman Archibald Stirling
Able Seaman Matthew Stuart
Steward Mark Stephens
Mar Eng Art Geoffrey Stockwell
L/Corporal Anthony Streatfield
Steward John Stroud
L/Corporal Philip Sweet
A/Weap Eng Art David Strickland
Able Seaman Adrian Sunderland
Corporal Paul Sullivan
Corporal Stephen Sykes
Sapper Wayne Tabard
Guardsman Ronald Tanbini
L/Corporal Christopher Thomas
Guardsman Glyn Thomas
L/Corporal Nicholas Thomas
Guardsman Raymond Thomas
Lieutenant David Tinker RN
Mne Eng Mech Stephen Tonkin
A/Cook Ian Turnbull
Corporal Andrew Uren
Petty Officer Colin Vickers
Corporal Laurence Watts
Guardsman James Weaver
Guardsman Andrew Walker
Corporal Edward Walpole
L/Corporal Christopher Ward
WO2 Daniel Wight
A/Ldg Marine Eng Mech Garry Whitford
Private Philip West
Sergeant Malcolm Wigley
A/Wea Eng Art Philip White
A/Ldg Mar Eng Mech Stephen White
Guardsman David Williams
Mne Eng Mech Gilbert Williams
Apprentice Ian Williams
Marine David Wilson
Corporal Scott Wilson
Captain David Wood

MERCHANT NAVY
Captain Ian H.North
John B. Dobson
Frank Foulkes
James Hughes
David R.S. Hawkins
Ernest N. Vickers

(Men lost during the earlier stages of the conflict are listed in Part One of this book)